AF580835

LAW
AND THE
SCHOOL PSYCHOLOGIST
CHALLENGE AND OPPORTUNITY

A SPECIAL ISSUE OF THE
JOURNAL OF SCHOOL PSYCHOLOGY

BARTELL CARDON PETER KURILOFF

University of Pennsylvania

Guest Co-Editors

BEEMAN N. PHILLIPS

Editor

HUMAN SCIENCES PRESS
72 Fifth Avenue
New York, N.Y. 10011

ISBN: 0-87705-280-8
LC: 68-52341

HUMAN SCIENCES PRESS
Subsidiary of BEHAVIORAL PUBLICATIONS
72 Fifth Avenue
New York, New York 10011

Printed in the United States of America.

Volume 13 Journal of School Psychology Number 4

1975

CONTENTS

JOURNAL OF SCHOOL PSYCHOLOGY, INC.: 1975

FOUNDERS AND SHAREHOLDERS

The *Journal of School Psychology* is published by a corporation established for this purpose. The stockholders listed below have provided the capital necessary to launch the project. As school psychologists and trainers of school psychologists, they are interested in professional development of school psychology to the extent of risking personal funds and providing management and editorial support. The editorial staff wishes to acknowledge this substantial contribution of their professional colleagues.

Journal of School Psychology
1975 • Vol. 13, No. 4

INTRODUCTION

Since the Supreme Court's famous decision in *Brown vs. Board of Education,* the courts have played an ever increasing role in the reform of educational practice. A veritable flood of suits, and legislation in response to suits, touches virtually every aspect of schooling. How has school psychology been affected by this increasing judicial involvement? This special issue attempts to provide some initial answers to this question.

Richard Mandel, lawyer and educational administrator, was asked to write as if he were delivering the introductory lecture of a basic law course designed especially for school psychologists. He discusses the general relationship between the legal and educational systems. In order to create a clear picture for non-legal professionals, he purposely simplifies the complexities which arise whenever judicial procedures are examined in their living socio-political context.

One crucial outcome of recent court decisions is the extension of the Fourteenth Amendment due process rights to parents of exceptional children and youth. What this means to school psychologists is examined in William Buss' dialogue between a school psychologist and a lawyer. Besides giving a complete picture of the procedural framework in which school psychologists will have to function in the future, this leading expert on due process and education begins to elaborate on the complexities which Richard Mandel purposefully oversimplifies.

Leon Gorlow, a due process hearing officer appointed after *PARC vs. Commonwealth of Pennsylvania* and a professor of psychology, describes how school psychologists have responded to their new role as expert witnesses. He delineates several principles that the effective school psychologist who faces this challenge will wish to consider. While the astute psychologist may wish to follow Gorlow's suggestions as a matter of professional pride and from a sense of legal responsibility, Leon Kamin's presentation framing the woeful history of the intellectual testing movement in this country should make us doubly conscious of the potential consequences of the misuses of the tools of our profession.

Theimer and Rupiper carry this Kamin theme further and show how the courts have recently reacted to the gross injustices that existed in the education and treatment of handicapped children. Although such litigation will help to insure the right of all children and youth to an education and equal protection under the law, they stress that implementation will be more effective if school psychologists and the education profession assume the responsibility.

Peter Kuriloff's work illustrates the impact of due process on the role choices of school psychologists, shows how social organizational factors can influence those choices and demonstrates how no choice is free from both professional risks and opportunities.

Virginia Bennett and Jack Bardon, both academic psychologists and recognized leaders within the specialty of school psychology, shift the focus from response of the individual psychologist to what professional organizations can do in the face of current and future legal demands. They raise important questions concerning certification and accountability, among other issues, from the point of view of people deeply committed to the elevation of the speciality.

Donald Bersoff, school psychologist and lawyer, deals with the often faced dilemma of ethical and legal conflicts. His presentation is centered around an exciting (?) day in the life of a school psychologist, a day which begins in glory but ends in shambles. He discusses why codes of ethics fail to provide adequate support for psychologists and offers remedial recommendations.

The issue is concluded by Bart Cardon who points to university preparation as a key ingredient in much of the conflict between law and the practicing school psychologist. His emphasis is upon the philosophical foundation of much psychological service in the schools and the predictable difficulties which ensue as a consequence. Suggestions are offered for significant change in how school psychologists are trained and educated.

For us, the act of drawing this issue together has resulted in a deepened sensitivity to the plight of the practicing school psychologist in the face of dramatically altered legal expectations. We extend our appreciation to those who in these pages have attempted to grapple with various related aspects of the interface of law and the practice of school psychology. Whatever else this special issue may be, it is a beginning in openly facing what can no longer be avoided—the need to adjust, to change, to grow.

Bartell W. Cardon, Guest Co-Editor
Peter J. Kuriloff, Guest Co-Editor
Beeman N. Phillips, Editor

Journal of School Psychology
1975 • Vol. 13, No. 4

THE LAW AND EDUCATION: A BRIEF OVERVIEW

RICHARD L. MANDEL

Miquon School
Miquon, Pennsylvania

Summary: The purpose of law is to control human behavior through the allocation of rights and responsibilities among individuals, groups, and organizations. Legal requirements affecting school psychologists have their source in state and federal constitutions, statutes, executive orders, administrative regulations, and court decisions. If psychologists do not understand the nature of the legal process and its impact upon schools, their autonomy and competence will be curtailed by alienation from a significant constraint upon the practice of their profession. A description of the sources of law affecting school psychology and the interrelationships among them may increase psychologists' affinity for, and potential control over, the legal process.

The law's purpose is to control human behavior, including, at times, the practice of school psychology. While external constraints are often viewed as unwelcome intrusions upon professional autonomy, understanding the legal process may give the psychologist a sense of the rationality of the legal process and also a sense of affiliation with it. The psychologist can ultimately attain increased power and control through the acquisition of knowledge concerning the role of law in education and the possibilities of using law to implement change relevant to the practice of his profession.

This article is concerned exclusively with public law, as distinguished from private law (such as contracts and professional codes of ethics) which persons use to govern their private conduct apart from the involvement of any government institution. A public law is a statement issued by a public authority for the purpose of controlling the behavior of individuals. Public law (hereinafter simply called "law") is usually made through a predefined, more or less formal process. The procedures by which a legislative statute, judicial decision, or school board regulation becomes law are examples of formal processes for promulgating a law. When the principal of a public school orally announces that a psychologist is to use a new system for communicating testing results to parents and teachers, the principal is promulgating law, even though the procedures followed are extremely informal. The broad definition of law may be unfamiliar to laymen, but it is increasingly accepted by attorneys who are sensitive to the growing impact of informal administrative law upon their clients.

The force of law lies in its ability to cause people to comply with its requirements, either out of a sense of moral obligation to obey the commands of an authority perceived as legitimate, out of fear of the sanctions which may be forthcoming as a result of noncompliance, or a combination of the two. A law often includes reference to formal sanctions for noncompliance. The sanctions may be explicit, or inexplicit, as in our example above wherein the psychologist understands that noncompliance with the new system will cause the principal to pursue appropriate procedures within the school district to secure compliance. There are no sanctions expressed or implied in constitutional provisions; constitutions are deliberately framed in a broad manner so that further specificity through legislative enactment—including the definition of sanctions—is required for their effectiveness.

By imposing obligations of obedience, a law necessarily allocates power and distributes rights and responsibilites among affected individuals and groups. If a law gives students access to certain kinds of records, it allocates responsibilities to the school authorities and rights to the students. By defining the behavior expected of certain individuals in certain circumstances, the law also defines roles. Professionals are often confused and angry with the promulgation or enforcement of a law affecting the practice of their profession because such a law is changing roles in a manner contrary to the professional's expectations as an individual, as a member of a professional group, and as a member of an organization. A school psychologist, for example, may find himself compelled by law to participate in an adversarial hearing concerning the placement of a child in a special program, even though the psychologist firmly believes that such an adversarial process is extremely ill-suited to reaching a professionally appropriate decision regarding the child's education.

SOURCES OF PUBLIC LAW

Federal Constitution. There are several kinds of public law: constitutions, statutes, executive orders, administrative regulations, and judicial decisions. Each type of law has general characteristics which distinguish it: the process by which it is made, the specificity with which it commands (which affects the extent of further interpretation required for effective application), and its breadth of application to individuals, groups, and institutions within society. The sources of law can be conceived in a hierarchical arrangement, with subordinate kinds of law having to be consistent with the parameters established by the superior kinds of law. Most familiar in this regard is the notion of constitutionality—that the federal constitution is the supreme law of the land and that all other law, including state constitutions, must conform to the requirements of the United States Constitution. The rules and regulations promulgated by an individual school, for example, must conform to the rules and regulations of the local school district, which must in turn be consistent with the rules and regulations of the state department of education, which must not conflict with the relevant statutes passed by the state's legislature, which must be in accord with the state's constitution, which cannot conflict with the United States Constitution.

As one moves down the hierarchy, the process for making a law becomes less complex and formal and the specificity of the law and its narrowness of application become correspondingly greater. There is a reason for this relationship. The very broad statements of a constitution establish basic allocations of rights and responsibilities within a society and contain those commands which are perceived as most fundamental to the nature of the society which the constitution governs. Constitutions have correspondingly broad applicability, affecting every individual and entity within the society in important ways. The procedure for amending a constitution is appropriately complex and highly formal in order to assure that the society's basic structure is not altered without extensive deliberation and widespread consensus. The commands of a constitution, however, are typically incapable of clear application to a situation without further refinement through the processes of legislation, adjudication, and administrative regulation. The due process and equal protection clauses of the United States Constitution state, "No state . . . shall . . . deprive any person of life, liberty, or property, without due process of law; nor deny to any person within its jurisdiction the equal protection of the laws" (U.S. Constitution, Amendment XIV, Sec. 1). These constitutional clauses have affected American public education in major ways; they have been applied to forbid discrimination of many kinds, to prevent unequal treatment, to require procedural fairness when sanctioning student and teacher conduct, and to apply the federal Bill of Rights to the public school context. Yet these clauses only become effective guarantors of specific rights as a result of a lengthy process of interpretation through law suits, legislation, and administrative regulation at the federal, state, and local school district levels of government.

As one moves down the hierarchy of law, commands tend to become more specific, the scope of their applicability tends to become narrower, and the process of law making becomes appropriately less complex and formal. As we move from broad constitutional statements to specific administrative rules, the likelihood of compliance also increases because the capacity of the law to speak in highly specific terms to the precise persons whose actions the law is designed to control increases. It is hard to know how to obey or enforce the equal protection clause of the United States Constitution, but it is comparatively easy to obey or enforce a rule which requires that a Spanish-speaking child only be tested by a psychologist who is fluent in Spanish. A law's position in the hierarchy does not refer to its importance or effectiveness in terms of affecting behavior, but to its relation in the legal process to other types or sources of law.

State Constitutions. In our country education is historically a state function, and the United States Constitution is silent as to any requirements relative to education *per se*. Through the due process and equal protection clauses quoted above, however, the states are restricted in the manner in which they perform any function, including education. The provision of educational services by the states must conform to these and all other relevant clauses of the federal constitution. Moreover, each state has its own constitution, and to the extent that a state constitution requires the state legislature to establish a system of education, defines the nature and purpose of that system, or places limitations on the manner in which a state can govern its citizens generally, the state constitution provides law which allocates rights and responsibilities among its citizens and between its citizens and their government relevant to education. For example, the Supreme Court of the United States has interpreted the United States Constitution as not requiring the states to provide equal resources for education in each shcool district (San Antonio Independent School District v. Rodriguez, Note 1), but the New Jersey Supreme Court has interpreted that state's own constitution as mandating a substantially greater equality than now exists among that state's school districts in terms of the resources available for education (Robinson v. Cahill, Note 2). It is not contrary to the federal constitution for a state to provide greater equality than the federal constitution requires; the New Jersey Supreme Court's decision regarding its state constitution is constitutional under federal law.

State Statutes. Most state constitutions require that the state's legislature establish a public school system. For example, the Pennsylvania Constitution provides, "The General Assembly shall provide for the maintenance and support of a thorough and efficient system of public education to serve the needs of the Commonwealth" (Pa. Const. Art. 3, Sec. 14). The state legislature acts through the promulgation of laws. For our purposes we can divide the laws affecting education into several overlapping categories. In the first category are those few laws which define the population which has rights and obligations regarding attendance at school: compulsory education laws, laws giving persons rights to attend school between certain ages or up to a certain level of achievement, laws granting a right to education to certain classes of persons with special educational needs.

The second category is laws establishing the state system of public education. It would be possible for the legislature to discharge its constitutionally compelled obligation to provide a system of public education by administering by itself a public school system. Bills could go through the legislative process determining the curriculum for the coming school year, the precise expenditures for each item for each school, the hiring and firing of staff, the discipline of students. Legislators could debate the relative merits of the open classroom versus more traditional teaching methods, of one eleventh-grade chemistry textbook versus another, of one battery of diagnostic tests versus another, and so on. The disadvantages of such a system are obvious: lack of efficiency, lack of flexibility, and lack of expertise applied to a dynamic and complex enterprise. Either the legislature would spend all its time administering the state's school system and have no time for other business, or the state's other business would be handled and the school system ignored. In either case, the legislature is a cumbersome and inexpert body when it comes to public education. It has its appropriate role to play in the defining of public policy, but it is not appropriate as an administrative body. The option which avoids this problem, and which every state legislature has used, is for the legislature to discharge its constitutionally imposed obligation by delegating its authority in educational matters to an administrative agency, a state department of education, and subordinate local school district agencies. Laws defining the powers and responsibilities of the key elements of the state's system of public education usually provide a state board of education, a state superintendent of schools, a state department of education, local school boards, local school district superintendents, and local school district staffs. The state's laws define the method of appointment and qualifications for various positions and the duties and responsibilities of the various components of the system. If there are certain problems which have arisen or are anticipated in the system. the legislature usually tries to provide for those. There are often laws dealing with conflicts of interest, budget-making procedures, business affairs, and relations between parts of the system. Finally, and most importantly, the legislature usually grants to educational agencies at the state and local level the power to make rules governing the activities of the persons and groups within their administrative authority, and provides that such rules shall have the force and effect of law. The grant of such rule-making authority is the *raison d'etre* of an administrative agency, for it allows the agency to use its expertise and to react to situations with appropriate flexibility in the best interests of the educational process.

A third category of laws affecting education are those which cover matters which could appropriately be handled through agency rule-making, but which some special interest group has successfully managed to cover through legislative enactment. While the provision of a law on a subject eliminates it from the exercise of the agency's greater expertise and flexibility, it also gives greater protection to the special interest involved. As a creature of the legislature, no state or local school authority can act in a manner contrary to the legislature's laws. Legislation in this category includes the teacher tenure laws; student rights regarding suspension and expulsion; laws requiring the schools to provide certain curricular content such as the salute to the flag, the Pledge of Allegiance, and observance of certain holidays; and provision of services to students in various special categories (e.g., vocational, physically handicapped, retarded).

A fourth category of laws affecting education are the finance formulae which are embodied in statutes in almost every state and allocate state funds to each school district in the state on a yearly basis. Most states have equalization formulae which take into account, more or less, the disparity of local resources available to the various school districts in the state. Groups with special interests, such as urban or rural education or handicapped children, often make the financial aid formulae their focus of attention, as the formulae can be adapted to provide funds earmarked for a special category of children.

The final category of state laws affecting education is broad and indefinite in scope, as it refers to any law which may incidentally affect education. The entire criminal code of a state, for example, is relevant to education insofar as school personnel or students may be arrested or convicted of a crime and the school authorities may be forced to decide what response is appropriate. The laws affecting business transactions and governmental activities may all become relevant to education. Laws expressing a strong public policy may also be influential in causing school authorities to take or not to take certain kinds of action regarding racial integration, unwed mothers, juvenile offenders, and many other matters.

State and Federal Administrative Regulations. State and local school agencies are limited in their authority by the acts of the legislature which created them, as well as by the state and federal constitutions. Within the scope of their authority, however, the education agencies can make law and can adjudicate disputes, the state agency's law being superior (because the state legislature says it is) to that of the local school district. Except insofar as constitutional rights of teachers and students may be involved, the education function is generally given a broader interpretation by the courts than it was in the past, and it would be unusual for a court to hold that a school board has acted *ultra vires,* in excess of its legislatively granted authority. Thus, school districts routinely are involved in activities directed at the physical and emotional health of the child, whereas in the past such activities were occasionally struck down as illegal.

Although the United States Constitution allocates responsibility for education to the states, the past decade has witnessed a tremendous increase in federal legislative and administrative involvement in education through the granting of conditional federal financial support to local school districts. Congress has enacted legislation and appropriated funds to assist districts in developing new programs and in meeting the needs of students with special educational requirements. The Office of Education is the federal administrative agency created by Congress to administer most of these special grant programs. If a school district wishes to receive federal funds, it must comply with the federal statutes and administrative regulations which establish the conditions to be met by participating districts. Congress' provision of funds for education thus provides the federal government with leverage to develop and enforce a national policy on education. Federal laws and regulations may not only affect the programs for which the funds are provided, but may also be designed to influence general school district operations. For example, Congress has recently used its leverage regarding the grant of funds to require all participating school districts to give students and parents access to student files (U.S. Public Law 93–380, 1974).

Executive Actions. The executive branch of government plays a role in affecting education through the development and initiation of legislative proposals, the submission of education budgets to the legislature, and the appointment of key officials to education agency positions. Because of an orientation to local autonomy in education matters, however, the states' governors and the president play only these indirect roles in the law-making process affecting education and do not themselves usually generate executive orders which directly affect the educational enterprise.

RIGHTS AND RESPONSIBILITIES OF PUBLIC EMPLOYEES

Each employee of state and local school agencies and each pupil in the public schools has several roles in the legal process. He is a citizen of the United States and the state and, therefore, can claim the protections of the state and federal constitutions and statutes from state activity affecting his life. This legal protection forms the basis of legal claims concerning matters such as academic freedom, student rights, and discrimination. The employee is also under contract with the school district and is limited by the terms of his contract, which often makes explicit reference to the state's education laws as part of the contract's terms. Since the employer is a state agency and not a private corporation, however, the employer cannot place any terms in the contract or act in any way regarding the employee which is contrary to the provisions of the state and federal constitutions regarding state action. For example, a public school district cannot prevent one of its psychologists from joining a group which is critical of the district's policies concerning the intelligence testing of minority students and speaking out on this issue, so long as the psychologist's activities do not disrupt the operations of the school system. A contractual provision which prohibited the psychologist from exercising his constitutional rights to free speech and association would be unconstitutional.

While constitutional provisions limiting state activity give the state employee certain rights which private employees do not have, they also impose parallel obligations: the public employee is himself the agent of a state, not of a mere private employer. As a state agent, the employee is restricted in his actions *vis a vis* other persons, such as subordinate employees, students, and parents. The same state and federal constitutional provisions which protect the employee from illegal actions by his employer thus also serve to limit his actions in the scope of his state employment. When a school board member, superintendent, principal, teacher, or school psychologist acts in a manner which deprives a student of his federal constitutional rights to due process prior to limiting his access to education, he has violated the United States Constitution and may not only be forced to change his behavior by a court, but also may be liable to the student whose rights he has harmed for money damages (Wood v. Strickland, Note 3). State statutes and administrative regulations also grant rights to, and require duties to be performed by, board members, employees, students, and parents.

JUDICIAL RESOLUTION OF CONFLICT

As we have seen, there are multiple sources of law, each generating many particular laws affecting the rights and obligations of individuals involved in public education. When there is a dispute regarding which of two or more conflicting laws is applicable to a situation or which of two or more interpretations of a law is correct, the judicial branch of government is available to disputants for resolution of their disagreement. If a student claims a right under regulation, statute, or constitution to a formal hearing prior to being suspended from public school and school officials claim that the student does not have such a right, then the courts, probably in a lawsuit brought by the student, must decide whether the laws which the student claim give him his right to a formal hearing do, in fact, grant such a right to the student and a corresponding obligation upon the school officials.

An individual, such as the suspended student in our example, or a group, organization, or governmental agency which believes that its rights under law have been or are about to be violated and that private settlement or negotiation will not result in adequate redress for the alleged wrong, can file a complaint in a court of law seeking government resolution of the dispute. The advantage of using the courts to settle a dispute is that the victorious party can enforce its verdict through the power of the government, which the courts will order into action against a defeated party which refuses to comply with the court's decision regarding the legal rights and obligations of the parties.

The party filing a complaint is the plaintiff and the party defending the lawsuit is the defendant. There may be multiple parties on either side of the lawsuit. The plaintiff must indicate in his complaint the nature of his claim, including a reference to the law which he claims grants him the right and imposes on the defendant the obligations which serve as the basis of the lawsuit. In many innovative lawsuits affecting education (for example, a lawsuit claiming that a student plaintiff's right to an education appropriate for a child with learning disabilities has been violated by a defendant school district) the case may turn on the question of whether the plaintiff's complaint refers to a legally recognizable right. If the plaintiff cannot convince the court that some constitutional provision, statute, or regulation gives him the educational right on which he is basing his lawsuit, then he loses his case without getting to trial. The plaintiff also must ask for some kind of remedy from the court which the court is capable of granting. Typical kinds of remedies include money damages to recompense the plaintiff for wrongs done to him, injunctions against the defendant compelling him to perform or to refrain from performing certain acts, or a mandamus (an order against a government official compelling him to perform an official act required by law).

Law cases usually begin in a trial court. After the parties have exchanged formal papers, called pleadings, which serve to define their positions relative to the lawsuit, there is an opportunity for the litigants to resolve the case without going to trial. This is accomplished through proceedings during which the parties disclose to one another the substance of their evidence and make arguments to the judge assigned to the case relative to their respective positions on the relevant law (the days of achieving justice through dramatic courtroom surprises are, alas, over). The case will not go to trial if the court decides that the pretrial proceedings reveal that the law is in favor of one of the parties and that there is no dispute suitable for resolution through trial, in which case the judge will decide the case himself. If the parties go to trial, each side has an opportunity to present evidence supporting its version of the relevant facts and an opportunity to make arguments supporting its version of the applicable law. The judge decides the legal questions and the jury decides the factual questions, unless the case is tried without a jury, in which case the judge performs both functions.

Any party which is dissatisfied with the outcome of the trial, and occasionally it can be parties on both sides of the lawsuit, has a right of appeal to a higher court. The parties file briefs and argue their case before an appellate court panel, the appellant trying to convince the court that the lower court judge made significant errors in his trying of the case which justify reversal of the lower court's verdict and the appellee (who is satisfied with the original verdict) trying to convince the appellate court of the correctness of the trial court's decision. While every judicial jurisdiction provides for at least one appeal as of right, some states and the federal judicial system also provide a third level in the judicial process, a higher appellate court, such as the United States Supreme Court, which will hear appeals only on certain kinds of issues or in certain kinds of cases.

Our federal system generates two parallel judicial systems: each state has its system of lower trial courts and one or more appellate courts, and the federal system has district courts in every state, circuit courts of appeals (each of which is the appellate court for the district courts in a group of states), and the United States Supreme Court. In addition, both the federal and state systems have special courts with limited jurisdiction over certain kinds of cases. The same factual situation can give rise to lawsuits in both the federal and state courts, although the parties and the courts usually follow procedures that avoid duplication of litigation and consolidate the lawsuits. For example, if a child is suing his school district because he has been diagnosed as being emotionally disturbed and the district refuses to provide him with an appropriate educational program, he may allege that his rights under some state education statutes have been violated and bring his case in a state court, or he may allege that his rights to equal protection under the federal constitution have been violated and bring his case to a federal court. In practice, he can allege violations of both rights in the same lawsuit and bring his lawsuit in either court, each of which would hear and decide the issue relative to his alleged rights under both claims.

JUDICIAL LAW-MAKING

When a court decides a case involving individual litigants, it determines what the law is that governs the particular stiuation involved in the lawsuit. The Anglo-American legal system does not consist of a set of clear and absolute rules which are capable of mechanical application to produce a judicial decision in a case. The words of constitutions, statutes, and regulations are ambiguous: situations arise calling for resolution which the original framers of the law did not anticipate, and a mechanical application of the words of the law, even if possible, can lead to unwise results which violate the law's spirit. The judicial process, therefore, uses reasoning which seeks to reach decisions based upon an analysis of the intent of the applicable law—what the legislators, administrators, or judges who made the law sought to accomplish by it. The search for the law's intent often involves consideration of the public policy reasons behind the law, and, at times, an analysis of the relative merits of two or more possible interpretations of the law in terms of their wisdom and their impact upon affected individuals. It is because of this method of legal reasoning that the courts are necessarily involved in law-making, rather than mere law applying.

In the process of deciding what the law is in a particular case, the courts utilize the hierarchy of law previously discussed. If the meaning of a state statute when applied to a situation gives rise to a result in conflict with the court's interpretation of the state or federal constitution, then the court exercises its power of judicial review to declare the state statute unconstitutional. The result of declaring a statute unconstitutional or an administrative regulation *ultra vires* is to make the statute or regulation null and void, either *in toto* or as applied to the kind of situation which is the subject of the lawsuit. This power of judicial review is an extremely potent one because it serves to nullify the acts of a coordinate branch of government, and it is generally exercised by the courts with great care and only when they cannot resolve the case on grounds less disruptive of the functioning of other branches of government. While the power of judicial review is one that often gives rise to criticism of the courts for usurping the authority of other branches of government, without its exercise there would be no orderly way for enforcing constitutional and statutory provisions; each branch of government would do whatever it thought the constitution allowed and each administrative agency would interpret the law in the way it thought best.

Each public body would have uncontrollable power to determine for itself what the law is.

Judges do not merely promulgate their decision in a case; all federal trial courts, some state trial courts, and all appellate courts issue formal, written opinions giving the reasoning behind the court's decision. The use of written opinions provides parties and persons not parties to lawsuits with information on how the law has been interpreted. If the law has been given a certain interpretation, persons can adapt their behavior so that it conforms to the law. Judicial reasoning relies, in part, on a respect for precedent: if a law has been interpreted in the past as giving rise to a certain result, a similar case should give rise to the same result. The use of precedent permits relative certainty in the meaning and application of the law so that people can guide their conduct in conformity with the law as interpreted by the courts. Lawyers arguing a case discuss relevant precedent to show that a result favorable to their client should be obtained. Because the facts of no two cases are precisely alike, however, there is often room for ample debate on what the relevant precedents are and how they should be interpreted in relation to the case. By writing their opinions, judges provide a source of law, a source of statements by public authorities promulgated for the purpose of controlling behavior, not only the behavior of the parties to the lawsuit but also the behavior of persons in like situations. When we refer, as we have throughout this article, to what the constitutions, statutes, and regulations say, we also by implication refer to what the courts say that these laws say. The courts in their capacity as interpreters and appliers of the law to a large extent determine what the law is in terms of its actual impact upon behavior.

CONCLUSION

The existence of a law does not serve to assure conformity to its terms. There are many laws which—through intent or ignorance—are more honored in the breach than in the observance. Difficulties in communicating a law to individuals responsible for compliance, group and organizational norms opposed to the mandated behavior, social conflict expressed through the existence of a law and significant opposition to it, individual needs not satisfied by obedience, a lack of resources to provide for conforming behavior—these variables all serve to mitigate the effectiveness of a law in terms of its capacity for controlling human behavior (Mandel, 1974). The intelligent use of the legal process as a strategy for change in education depends upon an assessment of the proposed change in light of these variables and in light of the characteristics of the legal process as a vehicle for change. The public nature of any effort to promulgate a law permits the mobilization of significant opposition. The application of external force may not be as effective as the utilization of persuasion within an organization or professional group. Increased understanding on the part of professionals of the dynamics by which the legal process does and can affect education will help to increase the effectiveness of law as an instrument of planned change in educational organizations.

REFERENCE NOTES

1. *San Antonio Independent School District vs. Rodriguez,* 411 U.S. 1 (1972).
2. *Robinson v. Cahill,* 62 NJ 463, 303 A. 2d (1973).
3. *Wood v. Strickland,* 420 U.S. 308, 95 S. Ct. 992 (1975).

REFERENCES

Mandel, R. Judicial decisions and organizational change in public schools. *Review,* 1974, *82*(2), 327–46.

Richard L. Mandel
Principal
Miquon School
Miquon, Pennsylvania 19452

Journal of School Psychology
1975 • Vol. 13, No. 4

WHAT PROCEDURAL DUE PROCESS MEANS TO A SCHOOL PSYCHOLOGIST: A DIALOGUE

WILLIAM BUSS

University of Iowa

Summary: Courts and the Congress have recently extended to school children safeguards encompassed by procedural due process in cases involving disciplinary suspensions and special education placements. The meaning of due process and its implications for psychologists are illustrated in a hypothetical dialogue between a constitutional lawyer and a school psychologist.

Lawyer: I understand you would like me to explain what due process in student classifications means to school psychologists.

School Psychologist: Right. As a starter, is it your impression that I will regard it as good news or bad news?

L: Both. It really depends on how you look at it. Let's come back to that point later. To begin, why don't you explain to me the way the system works now and I will then attempt to tell you how it would differ under a due process regime.

SP: All right. At the present time the process of classification might begin in a number of ways. The critical thing is that when certain signals or clues about a child's learning behavior are noticed a rather informal investigation would be made and that in turn might lead to a much more formalized screening of the child. For example, a teacher might notice that a particular student is simply not able to understand the material being studied even though all of the other students do and the teacher has made special efforts with the student in question. These observations might lead to consultation between the teacher and the school counselor, the school principal or school psychologist (depending upon the available resources and how the school is organized). These consultations might then lead to further observations by the teacher, to in-class observations by the counselor or school psychologist, and perhaps eventually to more testing and other more formal evaluative procedures. In the latter event a school psychologist would give a series of tests to the child, make a determination about the child's capacity, and recommend a special classification with certain special educational features. Ordinarily this recommendation would be accepted and acted upon by the school administration. At some appropriate point along the way the child's parent would be brought in and informed of the school's recommendation.

L: Let's pick up at the end of that. What exactly happens when the parent is brought in?

SP: Well, we would explain what we have done and why and what our conclusions are and what this means for the student's reassignment.

L: Suppose the parent is not convinced?

SP: That, of course, presents a bad situation for us because the parents' lack of cooperation can seriously undermine the best of educational programs. We attempt to explain to the parent that what we are proposing is in the child's best interest.

L: But what if the parent remains adamant? What do you do then?

SP: Usually we would carry out our recommended reassignment based on our own professional judgment and hope that the parent will accept our good faith and at least give us a change to deal with the situation. Sometimes, though, we will acquiesce in the parents' opposition despite our contrary best judgment. I am not sure that this is ever a good idea but in cases that might be regarded as involving "close" judgments the parents' opposition may be too significant a burden to overcome. In addition, there is undoubtedly a certain amount of accommodation to practical politics. If we have a parent who will scream and shout and make a big fuss, sometimes it is simply not worth the hassle even though it may be the child who suffers in the long run.

L: By beginning with this parental role, I can suggest one critical dimension in the procedure you described that would be altered by a due process regime. If the reclassification of a student must satisfy procedural due process, the parent would be entitled to some sort of hearing to challenge the school's judgment about the appropriate reclassification.

SP: In other words the parent is entitled to assert legal rights on behalf of the child that may operate in the child's worst interest.

L: You certainly put your finger on a soft spot although you exaggerate the point somewhat. It is the student's right which is being protected, but because of the student's minority and assumed lack of capacity the student's right must be safeguarded by some adult presumed to have the student's best interest at heart. Usually this is the parent, although it might be a nonparent guardian or in some unusual situations a guardian specially appointed by a court. Mr. Bumble (in *Oliver Twist*) once said, if the law supposes that a wife acts under the direction of her husband, "the law is a ass." Well, the law is not so much of an ass as to believe that parents always have their children's best interest at heart. All the law assumes is that the parent is the best we can do as a general proposition. Now occasionally there will be an apparent conflict of interest between child and adult and in such cases I think it would be appropriate for a court to appoint a special guardian to protect the child's interest in a case involving educational classifications.

SP: I noticed that you are saying what you think would be appropriate. Does that mean that the law has not clearly so provided?

L: That is exactly what I mean. But I should add that there has been some legal recognition of parent-student conflicts and of the need for a special guardian in such cases (*Heryford* v. *Parker,* Note 1: *Marsden* v. *Commonwealth,* Note 2; In re *Sippy,* Note 3; *White* v. *Osborne,* Note 4; Buss, Note 5; Buss, Kirp, & Kuriloff, 1975).

But let's not forget the exaggerated aspect of the observation you made a few minutes ago. You suggested, I think, that there was something inherently unreasonable about permitting a parent to act on behalf of a child when the parent's action–well-motivated or not–might turn out to be injurious to the child's interest. The point seems exaggerated because the parent, after all, is not unique in being an imperfect guardian of the child's interest. Those acting for the school, too, claim to act in the child's best interest and they too are subject to error and conflict of interest.

SP: Well, I certainly concede that point. I see many cases in which teachers appear to be motivated by their desire to remove a troublesome child from the classroom when my opinion is that the child's educational development would be best served by leaving that child in a regular classroom situation.

L: What do you do in such a case?

SP: I don't pretend to be a saint. I am operating in a system in which I must constantly make judgments about how I can use my professional expertise to bring about the greatest good for the greatest number. First of all, what would be best for a particular child in the abstract may be qualified by a particular teacher's contrary judgment. On the whole, a student is not going to do well in a classroom where the teacher is hostile to that student or believes that the student is too dumb to learn. Secondly, I must make judgments based on both the particular teacher and the particular student and, I probably should add, the particular school principal. In some situations a teacher who feels unable to cope with the student can be persuaded to the contrary with the appropriate consultation and assistance, and I encourage teachers in that direction when the student is not an extreme case and when I think some support for the teacher will actually be forthcoming. Thirdly, one has only a limited number of situations in which one can successfully resist the pressure from teachers and principals to obtain the reassignment of a particular student. I must make judgments which involve husbanding my limited resources so that they are available for those cases where the student most clearly needs to be kept in the regular classroom.

Just so you don't get the wrong idea, I want to make it clear that I am not talking about slanting test results or making an evaluation inconsistent with facts as I see them. I know that some of my colleagues have been charged with doing this, but I suspect it happens rather seldom, if at all. What I am talking about is a case where the objective evaluation would justify reclassification but where my own skepticism about the value of special classes and my own belief that moderately retarded children can be handled in a regular classroom lead me to believe a regular assignment is best despite the evaluation.

Why don't we return to the hearing you mentioned earlier. What would actually be required by procedural due process?

L: Unfortunately, I cannot give you a very simple answer.

SP: You mean this is another area where the law is not clear?

L: That is one way to put it. Actually, it is not so much that the law is unsettled as it is that what the law requires varies according to circumstances. It is sometimes said that due process requires "fundamental fairness." You can readily see that this is not a very precise concept. (See Buss, Note 5, 550–52.)

SP: I would have thought that the procedure we were already using was fundamentally fair.

L: I can see why you would say that, and it is certainly not clear that you are wrong. But in the cases that have been litigated the courts have required significantly more than is now provided as you describe it (*Mills* v. *Board of Education,* Note 6; *Pennsylvania Ass'n. for Retarded Children* v. *Commonwealth of Pennsylvania,* Note 7).

SP: Before you go on, I see that you are making a distinction between what is required in general by due process and what is required specifically by due process for student classification cases.

L: That is exactly correct. More often than not, getting a legal opinion about the law means getting an informed guess. It means taking several concrete starting points and extrapolating from them. For example, in talking about the requirements of procedural due process in student classification cases I would tend to base my opinion on four distinct starting points. I am sure that most other knowledgeable lawyers would be influenced by these same starting points, although there would be a great variety in exactly how these points were used and I am sure some lawyers would want to use additional reference points. My points of departure are two Supreme Court decisions and two groups of lower court decisions.

The first Supreme Court decision was made in a case called *Goldberg* v. *Kelly* (Note 8), involving the termination of welfare payments under a federal program called Aid for Families with Dependent Children. In that case the Supreme Court held that the welfare payments could not be terminated until the claimant had been given a hearing for which the claimant had prior notice and at which the claimant had the right to submit evidence to challenge the reason for termination, the right to cross-examine witnesses testifying for the government, the right to be represented by counsel, and the right to have a determination made by an impartial decision maker. This case is important because it involves more spelling out of the details of procedural due process than most other cases have done. In addition, *Goldberg* v. *Kelly* is expressly addressed to *minimal* procedural due process requirements; the Court made it very clear that the procedures there specified were tailored to *pre*-termination relief and that the welfare claimant denied a claim despite this prior hearing was entitled to more thoroughgoing procedures after termination. The second Supreme Court case, *Goss* v. *Lopez* (Note 9), involved a student suspension of 10 days or less. The Court, in that case, regarded such suspensions as significant enough to require procedural safeguards but mild enough to require only extremely minimal safeguards. Specifically, the court required that a student, before suspension, be notified of the charge of wrong doing, be given an opportunity to state his side of the story, be informed of the factual basis of the charge, and be given an opportunity to offer inconsistent or explanatory facts. In requiring only these very minimal protections, the court emphasized not only the relatively moderate nature of the short-term suspension as a sanction from the student's point of view, but also stressed heavily the great burden upon school administration if more exhaustive procedures were mandated for the very large number of short-term suspensions that are used.

Third, the lower federal courts, in a variety of expulsion and long-term suspension cases, have required procedures very much like those required by

Goldberg v. *Kelly*. They have sometimes expressly excluded some particular safeguard, such as the right to cross-examine (*Dixon* v. *Alabama Board of Education,* Note 10) or the right to counsel (*Madera* v. *Board of Education,* Note 11), but on the whole they have required that the student threatened with exclusion be given adequate notice of the charge against him and an opportunity to rebut or explain those charges (*Williams* v. *Dade Co. School Bd.,* Note 12; *Vail* v. *Board of Educ.,* Note 13; *Fielder* v. *Board of Educ.,* Note 14). Generally speaking, this opportunity to rebut or explain has entailed providing the student with full factual information about the case against him and with the means necessary to offer a defense—presentation of evidence, presentation of arguments, cross-examination, legal counsel, maintaining of record (*Black Coalition* v. *Portland School Dist.,* Note 15; *Marin* v. *University of Puerto Rico,* Note 16; *Givens* v. *Poe*, Note 17). Fourth, there have been two cases which explicitly deal with procedural rights in connection with student classification, *Pennsylvania Ass'n for Retarded Children* v. *Commonwealth* (Note 7) and *Mills* v. *Board of Educ.* (Note 6). Both of these cases held that a student could not be excluded from public schools by reason of having special education needs, that assignment in a regular class was the presumptively correct assignment, that the school had the burden of proof in establishing that some other assignment was correct, and that no student could be assigned to a special class or special school without a prior hearing at which due process was afforded. In substantial agreement, the courts in these two cases required the following procedural safeguards for the student:

1. Notice in advance of the hearing of the factual and theoretical basis of the proposed reclassification.
2. The right to submit evidence.
3. The right to cross-examine any witness supporting the school's position.
4. The right to be represented by a lawyer.
5. The right to have the case decided by an independent hearing officer.
6. The right to learn the details of the schools' position, including examination of the student's school records.
7. The right to state-provided independent psychological examination.

SP: You must realize that there is a great deal of detail in what you have stated. Is it possible to summarize it in any meaningful way?

L: Yes, I think it is. I think the essence of what these various benchmarks suggest is that a person who is about to be adversely affected by government action is entitled to notice of the basis of the government's action and an opportunity to respond to the government's position by way of proving contrary facts or additional facts that lead to a different conclusion or to reinterpret the total set of facts submitted by the government and/or the affected person so that a different conclusion seems appropriate. Everything else is supplementary to this basic purpose of the hearing. For example, a lawyer is permitted to represent the affected person because of the lawyer's skill in marshalling evidence with respect to a particular issue and because a lawyer is in a better position to determine what the affected person's best legal case is. Cross-examination is provided because that is a device which has proven itself over time as an effective means for uncovering testimonial error—whether based upon outright falsehood, incomplete statement of the truth, or merely misjudgment or faulty memory. An impartial decision maker is essential because the entire enterprise would be undermined if the person making the decision was unable or unwilling to discover the truth as it is developed at the hearing.

SP: That summary was very helpful, but now I would like to ask some more specific questions. Isn't there a great danger that the lawyer will simply make the whole procedure an adversary one?

L: That is always the first question asked, and of course it is a possibility. But I think the best answer is "possible but not likely." First of all, it is important to correct the unstated assumption that the procedure is non-adversarial without the lawyer. If we are talking about a situation in which the parent has demanded a hearing by reason of dissatisfaction with the school's classification, we are clearly talking about a situation in which the parties have adverse interests. The presence of the lawyer does not create the adversity. In fact, there is a very good chance that most reasonably competent lawyers will reduce the element of hostility or antagonism that is inevitably present in such a situation. Where the parent's interest is personal, the lawyer's is professional. More often than not, the lawyer will hurt his client's case by antagonizing those present, and a smart lawyer will surely know that. What the lawyer wants to do, because that is what he is paid to do, is to make sure that the decision maker sees the facts put together in some coherent order that might lead to a different conclusion from the one the school is proposing. The lawyer will do that best by presenting the matter in a detached fashion and in a way likely to attract some sympathy from the decision maker.

SP: You spoke of a right to a state-provided independent psychological examination. Would not that be more useful than a lawyer?

L: If you were creating priorities, in many cases—perhaps most cases—the independent psychologist would probably be more important than the lawyer. But we are not talking about one procedure or another. We are talking about using procedures which will provide the basis for a fair decision, and it seems clear to me that the lawyer and the psychologist both have important contributions to make to the student's case.

SP: When you talk about cross-examining witnesses, I assume that means that the school psychologist would be subjected to questioning by the student's lawyer.

L: That's correct.

SP: Does that mean that the school psychologist would be denied an opportunity to explain in his own words from a professional perspective how a particular judgment was reached?

L: No, it certainly should not mean that. First of all the school psychologist would initially testify on what is called "direct examination," presumably in response to questions by the lawyer representing the school. During this direct examination it would be quite appropriate for the lawyer to ask the school psychologist to explain the evaluation in the psychologist's own words in narrative form. Furthermore, even on cross-examination the student's lawyer would not have a totally free hand in the form of questioning. The hearing officer could and should prevent a question-and-answer sequence that thwarted the school psychologist's attempt to clarify and qualify answers of a yes and no variety.

SP: There is something that has been bothering me ever since we started talking about this hearing. You spoke of the central importance of notice and the right to respond and you spoke of the lawyer's training in organizing facts to answer some particular question. What questions are at issue at such a hearing?

L: That is a central question that sometimes gets forgotten. I think it is central because it helps to define the nature of the hearing and the procedures that should be available in it. I cannot list all of the open questions but I can at least suggest some of the important ones. First and foremost, the hearing would be designed to question any factual conclusion upon which the school's recommendation was based. To take a simple example, it would attempt to minimize the chance that information from the student's record had been erroneously copied. Second, the hearing would deal with the question of whether an appropriate test or tests had been administered. This, of course, would raise questions of professional judgment, and it is one of the places where an independent school psychologist testifying for the student would be important. Third, somewhat similarly, the interpretation of test results could be challenged. Fourth, the basis of the placement of the student would be open to question. In part this last question would deal with what the student's educational needs really were—it is the test interpretation issue in a broader form. Another aspect of this question of proper placement would be whether a particular proposed placement really was able to provide particular educational needs. In part, it would consider which of the two or more educational needs, and thus possibly which of two or more educational placements, is of paramount importance. Finally, it would deal in part with the question of whether noneducational considerations such as cost, proximity, and preference were and should be taken into account. Perhaps it is important to restate that these questions are answered both on the basis of factual information and on the basis of judgments applied to those facts; what is central and constant is the assumption that a better decision can be reached when two persons with distinct points of view assist in producing a factually accurate record and in drawing reasonable inferences from that record.

SP: Oh, that reminds me of a question I had earlier: Who is this hearing officer, anyway?

L: That is an important question but there is no simple answer to it. According to general principles of due process the hearing officer should be impartial (*Goldberg* v. *Kelly,* Note 8; *Morrissey* v. *Brewer,* Note 18). But impartiality is a relative thing and you can readily see that providing a hearing officer who is totally impartial is not easy. For example, it may be difficult to obtain a hearing officer who has no opinion about whether special classifications tend to be good or bad, accurate or inaccurate. General views of that kind are not legally disqualifying, but they certainly disturb any notion of dead-center impartiality.

SP: Are there other requirements for determining who the hearing officer should be?

L: I do not think there are other requirements clearly mandated by usual notions of due process, but it is obviously important that the hearing officer have some understanding of legal proceedings so that the hearing can be effectively run and so that the hearing officer and not the competing lawyers will remain in charge.

SP: Shouldn't the hearing officer be a school psychologist?

L: In the state of Pennsylvania, where there has been the most experience with procedures of this kind, most of the hearing officers have in fact been school psychologists or persons with training and expertise in special education. The advantage of having a school psychologist is obvious. He will understand the evaluative procedures that have been used and will be in a position to make an independent judgment about the correctness of the proposed recommendation. But there is a disadvantage as well. As I already suggested, the school psychologist will tend to see things in the same way as the person who has already made the primary decision for the school. In addition, school psychologists are not likely to be familiar with legal procedures.

The ideal, I suppose, would be a lawyer who is specially trained to understand the psychological procedures involved or a psychologist specially trained to understand the legal procedures involved (Buss, Kirp, & Kuriloff, 1975, 412–16). Obviously it will be quite a while before we have a pool of such experts readily available. In the meantime, any procedural due process hearings for student classifications will have to be presided over by hearing officers who are the best that can be found and who are trained to compensate for any deficiencies in background to the extent possible in relatively short time periods. If due process hearings do become generally required for classification decisions, it seems likely that both law schools and schools of education will have to give serious consideration to finding means to prepare the hearing officers.

SP: Well, I see some of the reservations that you have, but it seems totally impossible to me that anyone other than a school psychologist could make this important decision on the basis of what happens at this hearing.

L: I think the hearing officer's independent expertise is less important than appears at first because the student is entitled to use an independent expert in presenting his case. In my opinion, the lawyers and expert witnesses for the two sides can present the case in such a way that even an unexpert hearing officer will be able to make an informed judgment.

SP: The procedure you describe strikes me as being extremely time consuming and potentially expensive.

L: You are absolutely right about that, and that is an important cost of such procedures that should not be ignored. We do not yet have enough experience to make very definitive judgments, but I assume in the long run the procedure will be shaped to minimize unproductive expenditures of time and money. For example, if there is no clear gain to be had from oral questioning of the school psychologist, a written summary of his evaluation may be accepted. It is possible that approval of such written presentations may eventually be regarded as adequate as a matter of law, and in the meantime the hearing officer should have considerable discretion in determining just how much needs to be done through oral presentation and how much by written testimony. The trick is to get as much efficiency as possible without eliminating cross-examination where it really would be valuable. For example, if the conditions under which a particular test was administered were relevant in assessing the test results, it would certainly be desirable to subject the school psychologist to cross-examination with respect to these conditions.

SP: Once the hearing officer makes a decision, is that the end of the case?

L: Probably not. For example, an administrative appeal of the hearing officer's decision to the superintendent of public instruction is possible, as is provided in the system being developed in Pennsylvania. In addition, an appeal to the courts would often be available.

SP: Would this be the state courts or the federal courts?

L: It would ordinarily be the federal courts if the due process hearings are being held as a matter of the student's federal constitutional right and state courts if the hearings were based on state law.

SP: I am surprised to hear you say that. I thought we were talking about constitutional rights all this time.

L: I understand why you would say that, and perhaps I even led you to that conclusion myself. Due process is not only a fuzzy concept when used in the constitutional sense, it is also a concept used in many different senses. As a constitutional doctrine, it derives explicitly from the language of the fourteenth amendment (and also the fifth amendment), which prohibits action by government that deprives a person of life, liberty, or property without due process of law.

SP: That is interesting. What sort of a deprivation of life, liberty, or property is ever involved in a student classification case?

L: I must tell you frankly that it is still arguable that no constitutional deprivation at all is involved when a student is specially classified and assigned. The few lower federal courts that have dealt with this problem have simply assumed such a deprivation without much discussion, and it has not yet been resolved by the Supreme Court of the United States. I personally think there is a very strong argument that a classification case does involve a deprivation of both "liberty" and "property" as those terms are used in the fourteenth amendment.

It involves liberty in the sense that assigning a student to a special class definitely does restrict the student's freedom by limiting the student's future employment and educational opportunities. I realize that it is arguable that such a special assignment will in fact enhance a student's opportunities. That is, given the student's educational capacity, the special assignment will enable the student to obtain the most education and thus to maximize his potential in life. But the contrary argument is that assignment to special classes almost always means assignment to classes in which a less demanding education is provided and, partly because of the reduced educational demands and opportunities, special assignments are rarely reversible. Furthermore, it is clear that in the long run the student's assignment to a special education class will tend to limit his opportunity to obtain employment that pays well or has much status. These losses of opportunity are probably a result of the stigmatization of special classification as well as of the diluted educational program. The stigma of special classification also may be harmful in itself (*Goss* v. *Lopez,* Note 9; *Board of Regents* v. *Roth,* Note 19; *Wisconsin* v. *Constantineau,* Note 20; Kirp, Note 21, n. 44, p. 776). The important question to ask is not whether the assignment is right or wrong, in the student's best interest or not, but whether, from the point of view of the average student, special classification means expanding or contracting opportunity.

It is also arguable that a decision to classify a child as "special" would entail a deprivation of property in the constitutional sense. This, I suspect, will sound rather legalistic to you, and it is certainly true that it uses the concept of property in a very specialized fashion. The courts have said that property as used in the fourteenth amendment means a claim of entitlement that is created by the government at any level (*Board of Regents* v. *Roth,* Note 19). For example, a teacher with tenure has a property interest that entitles that teacher not to be discharged without satisfying the requirements of procedural due process. As I am using it here, a student's property interest would be based on the fact that the states have created a system of public schools and have made it a right under state law for every student to attend classes in these public schools. It seems reasonable to conclude that, in the absence of some specific determination that the student is lacking educational capacity, the right to attend public school classes entitles the student to attend regular classes in regular schools. Perhaps the easiest way to understand the property concept as it is used in this context is to point out that, within the framework of state law, it is not contemplated that a student could be excluded from regular classes simply because a school principal did not like that student. The student might be thought of as having a legal claim to attendance in a regular school that can be rejected only on the basis of establishing the existence of certain criteria such as those involved in making "special" classifications.

You understand that to say a liberty or property interest exists is not to say those interests are absolute rights or that they directly prevent the special classification; it is only to say that these interests may not be affected adversely except in a *manner* consistent with "due process of law."

SP: That is a pretty long answer about the constitutional basis of due process. What about the nonconstitutional basis?

L: You recall that I stated earlier that due process is sometimes said to mean fundamental fairness. That is true as a matter of constitutional law. But it is also true in the much looser sense that due process is sometimes used to mean what is fair. Particularly what is fair procedurally. Consequently, quite apart from any constitutional requirements, procedural safeguards may be mandated legislatively. For example, in the Education of the Handicapped Amendments of 1974 (Note 22), Congress required any state seeking federal grants under the plan to establish specified procedural safeguards for decisions concerning the identification, evaluation, and educational placement of handicapped children. Furthermore, a state or a department of public instruction or a school district could decide that certain procedural safeguards should be applied in classifying students because of the importance of such decisions and because it would not be fair seriously to affect a student in this way without procedural protection. According to this usage, "due process" might require more than the constitutional dimension of due process requires.

SP: At any rate, as I understand what you have said the Supreme Court of the United States has never itself held that classification proceedings must satisfy some particular procedural standards.

L: That is correct.

SP: Well, that state of uncertainty is not particularly reassuring. What did you have in mind earlier in suggesting that I might think due process was a positive development for the classification of children?

L: As I said before, that depends a little bit on your point of view. The primary purpose of due process is to improve the correctness of the decision being made, in this case the classification decision. As I view its likely impact, it will result in more testing and retesting, the use of more different specific tests and different types of tests, more personnel, and the making of more time available to carry out testing. I suspect that these are things which you would have advocated and that, although no one really questions their value, they often have not been implemented in the past because of lack of resources. If I am right, due process should tend to force the schools to do what most school psychologists have been saying they should do all along.

SP: I see your point and insofar as it has that effect it is good news.

L: Perhaps the biggest difference between the present system and the due process system is what we might call limiting the finality of professional judgment both in the sense of subjecting that judgment to a re-evaluation and in the sense of making parental objections to the judgment more significant. I do not know whether you would call that good or bad news.

SP: It is, of course, easier not to have one's judgments second-guessed. And it is even a little satisfying to the ego to know one's judgments are, for all practical purposes, final. But those are not matters of first importance. In fact, it is highly desirable to have an independent reassessment of a single person's evaluation. And it is probably positive, on the whole, to be forced to deal with parental challenges. I say these things partly because of the seriousness of the judgments involved and because none of us has much of a monopoly on what is ultimately true or what will ultimately work in dealing with children who do not learn easily on the basis of the more or less conventional approaches of the classroom. Furthermore, giving parents a right to challenge may in fact give us an opportunity to convince them of the soundness of the proposed decision we have made, and it may give them at least some chance to participate and to feel that they have had an opportunity to present their side of things.

L: The Supreme Court has frequently stated that due process requires not only fairness in fact but the appearance of fairness, and many people have observed that adverse decisions may be more acceptable to people who feel that they have had some input in the decision-making process.

SP: There is one final advantage that at least may be encouraged by due process. Insofar as we cannot justify our recommendation or even insofar as we are uncertain about it, we may be forced to work harder at providing the auxiliary services needed to make special education in the regular classroom more workable.

L: That conclusion may seem particularly likely, if, as some courts have held, the school has the burden of proving that a particular classification is appropriate.

SP: "Burden of proof" has always had a technical ring for me.

L: Your instincts are very good indeed. Burden of proof is an important part of the procedural framework for decision making. In simple terms, it means that, if the case is about even, the party with the burden of proof loses. But it also represents something more than a procedural device. Policy considerations clearly influence the placement of the burden of proof. For example, in the special classification area, it seems very likely that the courts have placed the burden of proof on the school because of a judgment that a child ought not be branded as "special" and limited to the special program on the basis of an iffy case.

SP: I can't quarrel with that. I believe we should continue to help a child with the best education possible–including supplementary services–in the regular classroom until it is clear that we cannot help him there any longer.

L: That is probably a good place to end, but I can't resist adding one observation: The more successful our schools are in dealing individually with different children of all types and degrees, the less relevant procedural due process is. If all children were always given what the educators like to call "individualized instruction," a claim for due process in connection with special education would be rare in the extreme.

SP: Perhaps procedural due process will push us in that direction.

L: Let us hope, anyway.

REFERENCE NOTES

1. *Heryford v. Parker,* 396 F.2d 393 (10th Cir. 1968).
2. *Marsden v. Commonwealth,* 352 Mass. 564, 227 N.E.2d 1 (1967).
3. *In re Sippy,* 97 A.2d 455 (D.C. Mun.Ct. of App. 1953).
4. *White v. Osborne,* 251 N.C. 56, 110 S.E.2d 449 (1959).
5. Buss, *Procedural Due Process for School Discipline: Probing the Constitutional Outline,* 119 U. Pa. L. Rev. 545 (1971).
6. *Mills v. Board of Education,* 348 F.Supp. 866 (D. D.C. 1972).
7. *Pennsylvania Ass'n for Retarded Children v. Commonwealth,* 334 F.Supp. 1257 (E.D. Pa. 1971); 343 F.Supp. 279 (E.D. Pa. 1972).
8. *Goldberg v. Kelly,* 397 U.S. 254 (1970).
9. *Goss v. Lopez,* 95 S.Ct. 729 (1975).
10. *Dixon v. Alabama Board of Education,* 294 F.2d 150 (5th Cir. 1961), cert. denied, 368 U.S. 930 (1961).
11. *Madera v. Board of Education,* 386 F.2d 778 (2d Cir. 1967), cert. denied, 390 U.S. 1058 (1968).
12. *Williams v. Dade Co. School Bd.,* 441 F.2d 299 (5th Cir. 1971).
13. *Vail v. Board of Education of Portsmouth School Dist.,* 354 F.Supp. 592 (D.N.H. 1973).
14. *Fielder v. Board of Education of School Dist. of Winnebago, Neb.,* 346 F.Supp. 722 (D. Neb. 1972).
15. *Black Coalition v. Portland School Dist. # 1,* 484 F.2d 1040 (9th Cir. 1973).
16. *Marin v. University of Puerto Rico,* 377 F.Supp. 613 (D. Puerto Rico 1974).
17. *Givens v. Poe,* 346 F.Supp. 202 (W.D. N.Car. 1972).
18. *Morrissey v. Brewer,* 408 U.S. 471 (1972).
19. *Board of Regents v. Roth,* 408 U.S. 564 (1972).
20. *Wisconsin v. Constantineau,* 400 U.S. 433 (1971).
21. Kirp, Schools as Sorters: *The Constitutional and Policy Implications of Student Classification,* 121 U. Pa. L. Rev. 705 (1973).
22. Education of the Handicapped Amendments of 1974, 20 U.S.C.A. § 1413 (a) (13).

REFERENCES

Buss, W., Kirp, D., & Kuriloff, P. Exploring procedural modes of special classification. In N. Hobbs (Ed.) *The Classification of Children* 386. San Francisco: Jossey-Bass, 1975.

William Buss
Professor of Law
University of Iowa
Iowa City, Iowa 52240

Journal of School Psychology
1975 · Vol. 13, No. 4

THE SCHOOL PSYCHOLOGIST AS EXPERT WITNESS IN DUE PROCESS HEARINGS

LEON GORLOW

The Pennsylvania State University

Summary: As a consequence of the Consent Agreement reached between the Pennsylvania Association for Retarded Children and the Commonwealth of Pennsylvania in the United States District Court for the Eastern District of Pennsylvania, school psychologists are finding themselves increasingly in the role of expert witness in due process hearings. The paper identifies a number of problems regarding the witness behavior of psychologists in these hearings and proposes some recommendations and resolutions.

It is now well known that the Pennsylvania Association for Retarded Children and the Commonwealth of Pennsylvania entered into an *Amended Consent Agreement* for Civil Action No. 71–42 in the United States District Court for the Eastern District of Pennsylvania. This amicable settlement detailed the manner in which retarded children would henceforth be assured equal protection of the law in the matter of their education. The *Amended Stipulation* in the same District Court, dated February 14, 1972, further elaborated and detailed for parents of retarded children within the Commonwealth their right to *due notice* and *due process* in respect to recommendations for change in the educational status of their children. The Amended Stipulation requires that notice of the change proposed by a school district be given in writing to the parent or guardian. In addition, it grants the parent or guardian the right to contest the proposed action at a hearing before the Secretary of Education or his designee. Over the recent past I have served as one of the designees of the Secretary of Education and have presided over what are known in Pennsylvania as Right to Education Due Process Hearings.

The hearing process is directed toward providing the hearing officer with the facts upon which he will endeavor to render a decision within the relevant law about the proper educational placement of a child. In the course of the meeting, officials of a given school district provide a statement of their recommendations with supporting expert testimony; parents present their contesting proposal with their own supporting expert witnesses. Attorneys acting in behalf of both parties may be and usually are present. The hearing officer provides an opportunity for the examination of all witnesses by opposing parties and seeks in his own interrogating of witnesses to uncover the essential and determining facts. The decision of the hearing officer may be appealed to the Secretary of Education.

Since the inception of the hearings program, approximately 150 hearings have been held in the Commonwealth before hearing officers, all of whom possess some specialized and relevant training in psychology. The Attorney General of Pennsylvania has endeavored to provide hearing officers with some minimal legal training in respect to the conduct of hearings. I have now presided over hearings in various parts of the Commonwealth and my remarks about psychologists as expert witnesses derive from my personal experience.

There is not a large body of literature which deals with the psychologist as expert witness. The early literature addressed the questions: Can a psychologist be construed as an expert witness? Rice's (1961) paper is an example, and it begins with the following question: "Is psychology sufficiently established at this time as a science to qualify its practitioners as expert witness . . . in federal and state courts . . . ?" This issue, of course, no longer poses a problem. As a result of the legal recognition lent to psychology by way of licensing and/or certifying statutes throughout the United States, there is now wide-spread acknowledgment within the law that psychologists do indeed qualify and may testify as experts (Pacht, Kuehn, Bussett, & Nash, 1973).

More recent literature deals with the nature of psychologist behavior in the witness role. Here also the literature is relatively sparse. A paper by Brodsky & Robey (1972) is a relevant example. The authors describe and examine two extremes of witness behavior engaged in by mental health professionals. They suggest that expert witnesses might be conceptualized as belonging to one of two groups: the *courtroom-oriented* witness group and the *courtroom-unfamiliar* witness group. The gist of their discussion is that courtroom-oriented witnesses behave in desirable ways while courtroom-unfamiliar witnesses behave in relatively undesirable ways. The former witnesses possess some legal training, have some knowledge of the law, have a minimal emotional reaction to subpoena, speak in clear and concise language avoiding jargon, and represent their position with mild advocacy. Courtroom-unfamiliar witnesses, as one might anticipate, have no relevant legal training, are unaware of law and evidence rules, show personal distress in response to subpoena, represent their findings in technical jargon and, often as not, respond with resentment and anger to cross-examination. Operating at the positive end of the implied continuum is viewed by Brodsky and Robey as leading to a more satisfactory collaboration between the law and the mental health professions.

In the future there will likely be an appreciable increase in literature dealing with psychologists as witnesses. Section 612(d) of Public Law 93–380 (United State Congress Education of the Handicapped Amendments of 1974 Part B) extends the right to due notice and to due process to parents of *all* handicapped children. As a result, a large body of material will accrue in the form of verbatim transcripts which will provide a data base for more systematic analyses of psychologists as expert witnesses. In fact, such research is currently being conducted by The Project on Student Classification and the Law, Graduate School of Education, University of Pennsylvania. The material which follows was, however, generated by relatively unsystematic observations during the course of due process hearings. It is impressionistic; it represents personal experience.

SOME OBSERVATIONS ON THE WITNESS BEHAVIOR OF PSYCHOLOGISTS

I have endeavored to record and react to a number of observations which have occasioned concern in me in respect to how adequately fellow psychologists appear to be discharging the witness function. In preparation for this essay, I reviewed the formal decisions I wrote for submission to the Pennsylvania Right to Education Office. The review constituted an aid in recalling the problematic witness behavior of psychologists testifying both in behalf of school districts and of parents. I reflect below on the issues as they arose in my review; I have not yet sought to classify the problems I have identified into reasonable categories.

1. School psychologists ought to present clear statements of the issues toward which their testimony is directed. The typical procedure at hearings is for counsel for the school district to ask the district's school psychologist to give an account of his psychological report in respect to the child under evaluation. All of us know that psychological report writing presents serious difficulties both in the use of language and in the designation of its presumed target audience. In a due process hearing, however, additional difficulty arises from the fact that psychological reports typically range over a large number of issues, not all of them relevant to the matter at hand. It would be useful to the hearing officer and to subsequent reviews of hearing officer decisions for a psychologist in the course of testimony to provide a clear statement of the issue he engages in his evaluation.

2. School psychologists ought to be knowledgeable about relevant sections of school codes (the bodies of State laws under which public schools function) which might limit their proposals. Problems arise when psychologists suggest courses of action or educational programs which are clearly at variance with relevant sections of such codes. I have had the experience of learning that some recommendations could in effect not be implemented because they were expressly forbidden by some section of the Pennsylvania School Code. For example, in a recent hearing a psychologist proposed placing a child whose IQ was within the average range into an educable mentally retarded class. Psychologists need to know their code so that their recommendations in respect to a child could not be exposed as illegal.

3. School psychologists also ought to be knowledgeable about the court decisions effecting their role. I have had the experience of psychologists developing recommendations which were clearly at variance with the Pennsylvania Amended Consent Decision. Psychologists in Pennsylvania who make recommendations about school placements for the retarded need to know, for example, how the Consent Decision rank orders placements in regard to what is most to least desirable, viz. " . . . among the alternative programs of education and training required by statute to be available, placement in a regular public school class is preferable to placement in a special public school class and placement in a special public school class is preferable to placement in any other type of program of education and training" (p. 4). Under such an agreement it is clearly not within the rules of the Amended Consent Agreement to recommend that a child above a certain minimal IQ score, for

example, be placed in a class for the retarded or that a child capable of tolerating group instruction within a school setting be given instruction in the home. It was stipulated in the Agreement, for example, that instruction in the home has low priority status among other possible educational programs. When a school psychologist recommends such instruction, he needs to be able to defend it as not just appropriate but as the *most* appropriate placement for a child. Without such a showing, the recommendation would not be in accord with the court decisions. The point I am making is that expert witnesses need to ground their recommendations in knowledge of the Consent Decision and the reduced degrees of freedom which result from it.

4. School psychologists ought to present themselves in their testimony as possessing a foundation in psychology as a science. It has caused me some dismay to discover that some psychologist witnesses have not been able to testify to such issues as the standard error of an obtained score or the fact that an obtained score has two components consisting of a true score and an error score. Since scores on psychological tests become important in the course of applying rules and regulations proceeding from statutes, it is of great importance that psychologists present their material with some statistical sophistication in this regard. I have also been concerned that psychologists are not giving adequate acknowledgment to the fact that while the error components in an array of scores are distributed randomly, the scores they obtain in specific instances may in fact be minimal scores. Inasmuch as scores on tests are intimately involved in special class assignment and lead to the placement of children in stigmatized classes, scores need to be interpreted with more care than they have been in my experience.

5. School psychologists ought to persuade the hearing officer and other observers that they have full and professional familiarity with the instruments they employed in arriving at their recommendations. It is a matter of some distress to me to observe psychologists testifying about their findings without basic knowledge about the construction, standardization population, validity, and reliability of the tests they used. Psychologists need to know and need to be prepared to testify that a given test, for example, may not be equitable in respect to assessing members of some minority groups or that the context of the examination itself may have served to yield scores which did not constitute a valid measure of the individual under view. In a recent hearing in which I presided a psychologist did not give due weight to the fact that extra test factors such as the difference in race existing between the examiner and the child may have acted to depress the true score. In addition, the psychologist could not provide the hearing with information regarding the standardization population.

6. School psychologist ought to be specific in respect to the educational program they recommend. Under the Consent Decision a burden is placed upon school districts to *specify* the educational plan for the child at issue. I observed psychologists proposing educational plans without specific content. On a number of occasions the educational plan advanced in the psychological report presented during the hearing is described as assignment to "an educable mentally retarded class." The main thrust of this observation is that psychologists need to specify the educational plan so that it can be under-

stood and examined in the course of the testimony. Lack of specific detail constitutes a disservice to the child.

7. A continuing problem in testimony derives from the fact that psychologists are either in the employ of the school district or in the employ of parents. This fact raises the problem of interest, bias, and partiality in testimony. All psychologists know the problem of bias in psychiatric testimony: we all believe that is is possible to field a number of psychiatric witnesses who will testify "white" and an equal number of psychiatric witnesses who will testify "black." The same problem exists in Right to Education Hearings. I have observed attorneys for both parties in a proceeding present an array of professional witnesses whose allegiances to agencies having a stake in the outcome have made me feel uncertain about their impartiality. It is a bothersome issue. Are there conditions under which psychologists might testify that could deal effectively with this important problem?

8. This latter point is related to the issue of credibility of witnesses. I have observed the full range of advocacy style from restrained and professional conduct on the one hand to anxious, fierce, and angry advocacy on the other hand. Needless to say, the stylistic aspects of witness behavior carry some weight in the judgment of the hearing officer. Brodsky and Robey quote MacDonald to the effect that "The medical witness should never take sides in a case, but should endeavor to be fair, impartial, and free from prejudice. He should regard himself as an independent witness for the court and should not act as an auxiliary advocate for the prosecution or the defense." While that position may be construed as ideal, I am not certain that it is desirable or even possible in our adversary system of justice. I do feel that this is an issue that will need to be addressed by psychologists who are going to be acting as expert witnesses. I am not sure that empaneling a body of experts who would act independently of the contesting parties would be a satisfactory resolution of this difficulty.

9. School psychologists ought to be willing to discharge the role of expert witness. In the course of my experience I have observed some psychologists display reluctance to state an expert opinion. They have simply sought to present what they understood to be the facts about the child under study without stating the conclusions which follow from those facts. I recall reeling on those occasions that psychologists adopting such a position were avoiding a fundamental responsibility. Psychologists testify as experts because they possess special knowledge beyond that of an observer. The expert in contrast to an observer "has something different to contribute. This is a power to draw inferences from the facts which a jury would not be competent to draw. . . ." (McCary, 1956, p. 8). The point I am making here is that since psychologists testify as experts, they need to fulfill the expert role and display a willingness to give testimony reflecting their best judgment. A related issue arises when a psychologist testifies that in his view all questions are unresolved. On one occasion a psychologist gave it as his view that there is *no evidence* under which he would conclude that a given child is plainly and unequivocably retarded.

10. School psychologists ought to have devoted an adequate amount of

time to studying the child under consideration. A problem which has occasioned some embarrassment to me as a psychologist arises when fellow psychologists are testifying to very important life plans having had minimal contact with a child. On several occasions psychologists under cross-examination by counsel have acknowledged that the extent of their contact with a given child has been minimal, over a period of say, one and a half hours, with no observation of the child in his natural environment. While many psychologists might want to argue that it is indeed possible to arrive at a set of recommendations after such minimal study, I am certain that many of us would share my dismay.

In concluding this essay it is worth noting that in the view of the Attorney General of the Commonwealth of Pennsylvania, the Consent Agreement and the Amended Stipulation require that the hearing officer act in behalf of the child's welfare. Hearing officers are not required to view the proceeding as an adversary event in which they need to decide between the position advanced by the parent and the position advanced by the school district. They may in fact recommend a third course of action which they judge to be in the best interests of a given child. In other words, hearing officers act for the child. In order to discharge their responsibility, hearing officers need to develop a complete record, and it is important finally to state that psychologists who will find themselves in proceedings of this kind will enhance their usefulness not only by attending to the issues identified in this paper but also by aiding in the development of a complete record.

REFERENCES

Brodsky, S. L., & Robey, A. On becoming an expert witness: Issues of orientation and effectiveness. *Professional Psychology,* **1972, 3,** 173–176.

MacDonald, J. M. *Psychiatry and the criminal.* (2nd Edition). Springfield, Illinois: Charles C Thomas, 1969.

McCary, J. L. The psychologist as an expert witness in court. *American Psychologist,* 1956, **11,** 8–13.

Pacht, A. R., Kuehn, J. K., Bassett, H. T., & Nash, M. M. The current status of the psychologist as expert witness. *Professional Psychology,* 1973, **4,** 409–413.

Rice, G. P. The psychologist as expert witness. *American Psychologist,* 1961, **16,** 691–692.

Leon Gorlow
Professor of Psychology
The Pennsylvania State University
University Park, Pennsylvania 16802

Journal of School Psychology
1975 • Vol. 13, No. 4

SOCIAL AND LEGAL CONSEQUENCES OF I.Q. TESTS AS CLASSIFICATION INSTRUMENTS: SOME WARNINGS FROM OUR PAST

LEON J. KAMIN

Princeton University

Summary: Social science instruments are not neutral. The concepts they are imbedded in, the aspects of reality they enable us to see, all have social and political consequences. That school psychologists need to pay close attention to the sociopolitical implications of their assessment instruments is illustrated through the woeful history of the use and misuse of the concept of intelligence in the United States during the first third of this century.

A growing body of scientific opinion calls attention to the role scientific instruments play in shaping human perception and therefore, human experience (Peirce, 1958; Dewey & Bently, 1960; Hanson, 1958; Kuhn, 1970). This view suggests that our instruments–be they our assumptions about human nature, the Iowa Achievement tests, or our concepts of intelligence–in large measure determine not only how we see students, but also how we feel and act toward them. It means that social science instruments such as intelligence tests, no matter how scientific they appear, are not neutral. If this argument is tenable it would behoove school psychologists to pay a great deal of attention to their use of assessment instruments in order to insure that the consequences they entail are socially constructive.

This paper illustrates the social impact of one of school psychology's key instruments by describing some of the social and political background out of which the intelligence movement in the United States took shape–and to which, in no small measure, it contributed. The conclusion reached is this: Since its introduction to America, the intelligence test has been used more or less consciously as an instrument of oppression against the underprivileged–the poor, the foreign-born, and racial minorities.

The first usable test of general intelligence was published by Binet in 1905. Though Binet protested against the "brutal pessimism" of those who regarded the test score as a fixed quantity and prescribed corrective courses in "mental orthopedics" for those with low test scores, the orientation of the American importers of Binet's test was very different. The major translators and importers of the test in the decade following Binet's publication were Lewis Terman at Stanford, Robert Yerkes at Harvard, and Henry Goddard at Vineland, New Jersey. These pioneers of the mental testing movement shared a number of sociopolitical views, as exemplified by their joint involvement in

This article is an abridgement and extension of material taken from Leon J. Kamin's *The Science and Politics of I.Q.*, Hillsdale, New Jersey: Lawrence Erlbaum Associates, Inc., Publishers, 1974. Reproduced with permission.

the turn-of-the-century eugneics movements. Perhaps a few quotations from their writings will make the point.

Terman, in his book (Terman, 1916) which introduced the Stanford-Binet test, after describing the poor test performance of a pair of Indian and Mexican children, wrote the following:

> Their dullness seems to be racial, or at least inherent in the family stocks from which they come. The fact that one meets this type with such extrordinary frequency among Indians, Mexicans, and negroes suggests quite forcibly that the whole question of racial differences in mental traits will have to be taken up anew . . . there will be discovered enormously significant racial differences . . . which cannot be wiped out by any scheme of mental culture.
>
> Children of this group should be segregated in special classes . . . They cannot master abstractions, but they can often be made efficient workers . . . . There is no possibility at present of convincing society that they should not be allowed to reproduce . . . they constitute a grave problem because of their unusually prolific breeding (p. 6).

Professor Terman should not be thought of as a racist. His stern eugenical judgment was applied even-handedly to poor people of all colors. Writing under the heading "The Menace of Feeble-Mindedness" (Terman, 1917), he declared:

> . . .Only recently have we begun to recognize how serious a menace it is to the social, economic, and moral welfare of the state . . . it is responsible . . . for the majority of cases of chronic and semi-chronic pauperism . . . organized charities . . . often contribute to the survival of individuals who would otherwise not be able to live and reproduce . . . .If we would preserve our state for a class of people worthy to possess it, we must prevent, as far as possible, the propagation of mental degenerates . . . the increasing spawn of degeneracy (p. 7).

The squandering of charitable moneys on the degenerate poor similarly caught the attention of Henry Goddard (1920) who lectured to a Princeton audience on the new science of "mental levels." That new science, he pointed out, had invalidated the arguments of gentlemen socialists who "in their ultra altruistic and humane attitude" were embarrassed that their own shoes cost $12, while those of a laborer cost only $3.

> Now the fact is, *that workman* may have a ten year intelligence while you have a twenty. To demand for him such a home as you enjoy is as absurd as it would be to insist that every laborer should receive a graduate fellowship. How can there be such a thing as social equality with this wide range of mental capacity?
>
> . . . .The man of intelligence has spent his money wisely, has saved until he has enough to provide for his needs in case of sickness, while the man of low intelligence, no matter how much money he would have earned, would have spent much of it foolishly. . . . During the past year, the coal miners in certain parts of the country have earned more money than the operators and yet today when the mines shut down for a time, those people are the first to suffer. They did not save anything, although their whole life has taught them that mining is an irregular thing and that . . . they should save . . . (p. 8).

To be diagnosed as "feeble-minded" was not a light matter in a period when discriminations between the criminal, the poor, the insane, and the dull were not clearly drawn. The public institutions to provide for such degenerates were in many states administered by a single functionary, the "Commissioner of Charities and Corrections." Further, prodded by the eugenicists, many states passed laws providing for the compulsory sterilization of the inmates of such taxpayer-supported institutions before their release. The preamble of the first such law, passed by Indiana in 1907, was typical in its assertion:

Whereas, heredity plays a most important part in the transmission of crime, idiocy, and imbecility." To this list of genetically determined traits, the New Jersey legislature added in 1911 "feeble-mindedness, epilepsy . . . and other defects," and Iowa in 1913 contributed ". . . lunatics, drunkards, drug fiends . . . moral and sexual perverts, and diseased and degenerate persons . . ."

The lot of those officially diagnosed as feeble-minded was not enviable, and it is of interest to read Yerkes' caution: ". . . never should such a diagnosis be made on the IQ alone . . . . We must inquire further into the subject's economic history. What is his occupation; his pay . . . we must learn what we can about his immediate family. What is the economic status or occupation of the parents? . . . When . . . this information has been collected . . . the psychologist may be of great value in getting the subject into the most suitable place in society . . . "(Yerkes, 1923, p. 8).

The genetic interpretation of socioeconomic class differences in test scores, fostered by Terman, Goddard, and Yerkes, could clearly serve to legitimize the existing social order. Perhaps the first major practical effect of the testing movement, however, lay in its contribution to the passage and rationalization of the overtly racist immigration law of 1924. This disgraceful chapter in the history of American psychology is not without contemporary relevance.

Prior to World War I, though certain classes of undesirables were excluded, there was no numerical limitation on immigration to the United States, nor were geographic distinctions drawn among European countries. But as early as 1912 the U. S. Public Health Service invited Henry Goddard to Ellis Island to apply the new mental tests to arriving European immigrants. Goddard reported that, based upon his examination of the "great mass of average immigrants," 83% of Jews, 80% of Hungarians, 79% of Italians, and 87% of Russians were "feeble-minded" (Goddard, 1913). He was able to report in 1917 that the use of mental tests "for the detection of feeble-minded aliens" had vastly increased the number of aliens deported.

The significance of these scientific findings was not lost upon the members of the Eugenics Research Association, who in 1917 appointed Yerkes as chairman of their "Committee on Inheritance of Mental Traits." The biologist Harry Laughlin (Laughlin, 1917), secretary of the Association and editor of its journal *Eugenic News,* wrote under the heading "The New Immigration Law": "When the knowledge of the existence of this science (mental testing) becomes generally known in Congress, that body will then be expected to apply the direct and logical test . . . (p. 22)."

Within months American entry into the war had brought the science of mental testing to a new level of public recognition. Intelligence tests were applied to some 2,000,000 draftees—under the direction of Colonel Robert M. Yerkes, with the assistance of many of the leading experimental psychologists. The influence of Yerkes may perhaps be detected in the massive influx of leading experimentalists into the Eugenics Research Assoication in 1920.

But in any event, the results of the Army's testing program were published, under Yerkes' editorship, by the National Academy of Sciences in 1921 (National Academy of Sciences, 1921). The data provided the first large-scale evidence that blacks scored lower than whites. But the chapter of most immediate significance in 1921 was that on the foreign-born. The test performance of immigrant draftees was analyzed by country of origin. The data were succinctly summarized: "The Latin and Slavic countries stand low." The Poles, it was reported, did not score significantly higher than the blacks.

These scientific data speedily became "generally known in Congress," with the considerable assistance of the scientists of the Eugenics Research Association and of Yerkes, now employed by the National Research Council. The secretary of the E.R.A. was appointed "Expert Eugenics Affairs Agent" of the House Committee on Immigration and Naturalization of the U. S. Congress; in 1923 the psychological and biological scientists of the E.R.A. elected as their organization's chairman the Honorable Albert Johnson. That gentleman, by a fortunate coincidence, was the congressman who chaired the House Committee on Immigration and Naturalization. Meanwhile, under Yerkes' leadership, the N.R.C.'s Division of Anthropology and Psychology established a Committee on Scientific Problems of Human Migration. That committee, in an effort to take the national debate over immigration "out of politics" and to place it on "a scientific basis," began to support relevant research. The first research supported was that of Carl Brigham, then Assistant Professor of Psychology at Princeton; he wrote *A Study of American Intelligence* (Brigham, 1923) with a forward by Yerkes praising the book's contribution to the scientific study of immigration.

The unique contribution of Brigham's book was an intensive reanalysis of the Army data on immigrants. Brigham demonstrated that, pooling across all countries of origin, immigrants who had been in the country 16 to 20 years before being tested were as bright as native-born Americans and that immigrants who had been in America only 0 to 5 years when tested were virtually feeble-minded. "We must assume," Brigham wrote, "that we are measuring *native or inborn intelligence.*" The psychologists who devised the tests had, after all, constructed special tests for the illiterate. The explanation for the correlation of test score with years of American residence proved to be simple. Twenty years earlier, immigrants had flowed into the country from England, Scandinavia, Germany; five or ten years before the war the massive "New Immigration" from southeastern Europe had begun—Italians, Poles, Russians, Jews. The decline of immigrant intelligence, Brigham noted, paralleled precisely the decrease in the amount of "Nordic blood" and the increase in the amount of "Alpine" and "Mediterranean" blood in the immigrant stream—a nice example of the power of correlational analysis as applied to intelligence test data. The Jew, Brigham declared, "is an Alpine Slav." The concluding paragraphs of Brigham's book pointed out that:

> . . . we are incorporating the negro into our racial stock, while all of Europe is comparatively free from this taint . . . .The steps that should be taken . . . must of course be dictated by science and not by political expediency . . . .And the

revision of the immigration and naturalization laws will only afford a slight relief. . . .The really important steps are those looking toward the prevention of the continued propagation of defective strains in the present population" (p. 210).

With this contribution behind him, Brigham moved on to the secretaryship of the College Entrance Examination Board, where he devised and developed the Scholastic Aptitude Test, and, at length, to the secretaryship of the American Psychological Association.

The political usage of Brigham's book and of Army data was immediate and intense. The book and the data figured prominently and repeatedly in Congressional committee hearings and debates on the new immigration law. I cite only a very few examples.

Dr. Arthur Sweeney, to the House Committee, January 24, 1923:

> The fact that the immigrants are illiterate or unable to understand the English language is not an obstacle. . . . "Beta" . . . is entirely objective. . . . We . . . strenuously object to immigration from Italy . . . Russia . . . Poland . . . Greece . . . Turkey. The Slavic and Latin countries show a marked contrast in intelligence with the western and northern European group . . . we shall degenerate to the level of the Slav and Latin races . . . (pp. 589–594).

Mr. Francis Kinnicutt, to the Senate Committee, February 20, 1923:

> The immigration from (Poland and Russia) consists largely of the Hebrew elements . . . some of their labor unions are among the most radical in the whole country . . . .The recent Army tests show . . . these classes rank far below the average intelligence . . . . See "A Study of American Intelligence" by Carl C. Brigham . . .Col. Robert M. Yerkes . . . vouches for this book, and he speaks in the highest terms of Prof. Carl C. Brigham, now assistant professor of psychology in Princeton University (pp. 80–81).

Mr. Madison Grant, to the Senate Committee, January 10, 1924:

> The country at large has been greatly impressed by . . . the Army intelligence tests . . . carefully analyzed by . . . Yerkes . . . (and Brigham). The experts . . . believe . . . the tests give as accurate a measure of intelligence as is possible. . . . The questions . . . were selected with a view to measuring innate ability . . . had mental tests been in operation . . . over 6,000,000 aliens now living in this country . . . would never have been admitted . . . (p. 837).

The Congress passed in 1924 a law not only restricting the total *number* of immigrants, but also assigning "*national origin quotas.*" That is, immigrants from any European country would be allowed entry into America only to the proportionate extent that their countrymen was already represented in the American population—*as determined by the census of 1890.* The Congressional proponents of the law frankly asserted that the 1890 (rather than the 1920) census was used in order to curtail biologically inferior immigration from southeastern Europe. That is the law which contributed utimately to the deaths of tens of thousands of victims of Nazi terror, denied entry to the United States because the "German quota" was filled, though other quotas were undersubscribed.

The biological partitioning of the European continent did not appease some ardent intelligence testers, who continued to perform relevant research.

Nathaniel Hirsch's work (Hirsch, 1926) was also supported by the National Research Council. To demonstrate the genetic basis of low IQ's in immigrant stock, Hirsch tested the native-born *children* of immigrants. He reported in the 1926 *Genetic Psychology Monographs*:

> That part of the law which has to do with the non-quota immigrants should be modified . . . .All mental testing upon children of Spanish-American descent has shown that the average intelligence of this group is even lower than the average intelligence of the Portuguese and Negro children . . . in this study. Yet Mexicans are flowing into the country . . . .
>
> From Canada . . . we are getting . . . the less intelligent of working-class people . . . the increase in the number of French Canadians is alarming. Whole New England villages and towns are filled with them. The average intelligence of the French Canadian group in our data approaches the level of the average Negro intelligence.
>
> I have seen gatherings of the foreign-born in which narrow and sloping foreheads were the rule . . . .In every face there was something wrong–lips thick, mouth coarse . . . chin poorly formed . . . sugar-loaf heads . . . goose-bill noses . . . a set of skew-molds discarded by the Creator . . . .Immigration officials . . . report vast troubles in extracting the truth from certain brunette nationalities" (p. 28).

That was the voice of Genetic Psychology Monographs in 1926. What shall we say of the voices of today's mental testers? The moral of this history seems to me sufficiently clear–and contemporary developments in mental testing too well known to us all–for explicit comment to be necessary. From this much, however, I cannot forebear. If we look closely at educational practices which have intellectual classification as their starting point, comparing them with the historical social practices based upon intelligence test data, we note uncomfortable similarities. School psychologists would be remiss, in light of warnings from our past, not to question the assumptions and predictable consequences of current classification and placement practices. To fail to do so is irresponsible at best, damning at worst. In light of recent court decisions discussed elsewhere in this special issue, such a failure may also prove fraught with serious personal risks.

REFERENCES

Brigham, C. C. *A study of American intelligence.* Princeton: Princeton University Press, 1923.

Dewey, J., & Bently, A. *Knowing and the known.* Boston: Beacon Press, 1960.

Goddard, H. H. Mental tests and the immigrant. *Juvenile Delinquency,* 1917, 2, 243–277.

Goddard, H. H. The Binet tests in relation to immigration. *Journal of Psycho-asthenics,* 1913, **18**, 105–107.

Goddard, H. H. *Human efficiency and levels of intelligence.* Princeton: Princeton University Press, 1920.

Hanson, N. R. *Patterns of discovery.* Cambridge, England: Cambridge University Press, 1958.

Hirsch, N. D. M. A study of natio-racial mental differences. *Genetic Psychology Monographs,* 1925, *1* (Whole Nos. 3 and 4).

Kuhn, T. S. *Structure of Scientific Revolutions* (Vol. 1, No. 2). Chicago: University of Chicago Press, 1970.

Laughlin, H. H. The new immigration law. *Eugenic News,* 1917, *2,* 22.

National Academy of Sciences. *Memoirs,* 1921, 15.
Peirce, C. S. How to make our ideas clear. *Selected writings.* New York: Dover, 1958.
Terman, L. M. *The measurement of intelligence.* Boston: Houghton-Mifflin, 1916.
Terman, L. M. Feeble-minded children in the public schools of California. *School and Society,* 1917, *5,* 161–165.
Yerkes, R. M., & Foster, J. C. *A point scale for measuring mental ability.* Baltimore: Warwick and York, 1923.

Leon J. Kamin
Professor of Psychology
Princeton University
Princeton, New Jersey 08540

Journal of School Psychology
1975 • Vol. 13, No. 4

SPECIAL EDUCATION LITIGATION AND SCHOOL PSYCHOLOGY

R. KAYE THEIMER
Tulsa, Oklahoma

OMER J. RUPIPER
University of Oklahoma

Summary: When constitutional or statutory rights of exceptional children were violated, litigation was implemented as one means to obtain those rights. Legislative and administrative actions were exhausted before the issue was brought to the courts. The procedure of litigation was first initiated in 1967, and several landmark cases since then have provided prototypes for subsequent cases which concerned the rights of handicapped children. As a result of the gross injustice that existed in the education and treatment of handicapped children, there were over thirty lawsuits filed on their behalf. Education and treatment of the handicapped child, long viewed as a charitable endeavor, must now be considered as an inalienable right not to be denied to the "special" citizen. Although the courts have been forced to decide upon some of the critical issues regarding exceptional children, the implementation will be more effective and efficient if the education profession itself assumes the responsibility. This overview of significant litigation points up the evidence presented in the lawsuits which should be of concern to the practice of school psychology.

The legal rights of many children and youth have been unclear and, at worst, ignored. Recently the atmosphere has dramatically changed as the result of scores of cases brought to court on behalf of "exceptional" children and youth. The central role of the school psychologist in educational matters pertaining to this group makes it imperative that the recent decisions of the courts be known and understood. The purpose of this paper is to provide an overview of significant litigation which directly concerns the practice of school psychology. Except in those instances indicated to the contrary, the courts have ruled in favor of the plaintiffs.

RIGHT TO EDUCATION

On January 7, 1971, 14 retarded children with the Pennsylvania Association for Retarded Children (P.A.R.C.) sued for themselves and for all the retarded children in Pennsylvania, or in legal terms "all others similarly situated," who had been denied equal access to education. *Pennsylvania Association for Retarded Children* v.*Commonwealth of Pennsylvania* (Note 1) was the landmark case in the right to education lawsuits that followed. The defendants were the state secretaries of education and public welfare, the state board of education, and thirteen school districts.

This paper is an adaptation of a doctoral dissertation completed by R. Kaye Theimer under the direction of Omer J. Rupiper, major professor, The University of Oklahoma, 1974.

The Pennsylvania School Code provides an education to all children and includes the exceptional. Despite this, large numbers of retarded children have been denied access to schooling (Gilhool, 1973). The plaintiffs charged that they represented as many as 53,000 people (Cohen and DeYoung, 1973).

The suit, heard by a three-judge panel, questioned public policy as expressed in law regarding the denial of free access to educational opportunities to the mentally retarded of school age. After following the testimony of four expert witnesses, the defendants called a halt and announced they wished to settle the case.

The October, 1971, injunction required that:

1. To provide as soon as possible but in no event later than September 1, 1972, to every retarded person between the ages of six and twenty-one, access to a free public program of education and training appropriate to his learning capacities.
2. To provide as soon as possible but in no event later than September 1, 1972, wherever defendants provide a pre-school program of education and training for children aged less than six years of age, access to a free, public program of education and training appropriate to his learning capacities to every mentally retarded child of the same age.
3. The Secretary of Education shall be responsible for assuring that every mentally retarded child is placed in a program of education and training appropriate to his learning capacities, and to that end . . . he shall be informed as to the identity, condition, and educational status of every mentally retarded child within the various school districts.

In order to assure prompt and expedient implementation, the consent agreement required the state to develop a plan for finding retarded children and a plan for providing educational opportunities and services. It required a notice to parents of retarded children of the court action. To facilitate quick action, the court appointed two Masters from the field of education and law, who represented the court in carrying out orders and injunctions. These orders were to be completed by September, 1972, when all retarded children between the ages of six and 21 were to be provided a publicly-supported education. On May 5, 1972, the June and October decrees were approved and adopted and were put into full effect.

Thus, judicial recognition had been made that all children are educable, and that all retarded children should have access to the benefits of public school. Those who have disputed this decision have taken the position that such an implementation would cost more than is beneficial.

Another landmark decision was reached in *Mills* v. *Board of Education* (Note 2). The parents and guardians of seven District of Columbia children brought this class action suit against the District for failure to provide a free public school education. The defendants answered that the reason they failed to provide such an education was the lack of necessary fiscal resources.

On August 1, 1972, Judge Joseph C. Waddy issued a final order and opinion in which he supported all the arguments brought by the plaintiffs. This decision applied to all handicapped children and not just a single category. The *Mills* (Note 2) case expanded the principles of the *Pennsylvania Association for Retarded Children* v. *Commonwealth of Pennsylvania* (Note 1) to all handicapping conditions and while P.A.R.C. was decided upon by a consent agreement, the *Mills* (Note 2) case provided a constitutional holding reached by a Federal judge in a contested case and set even a stronger precedent (Mental Health Law Project, 1973).

Judge Waddy held that the defendants could not be excused by a claim of insufficient funds. He stated:

> If sufficient funds are not available to finance all of the services and programs that are needed in the system then the available funds must be expended equitably in such a manner that no child is entirely excluded from a publicly supported education consistent with his needs and ability to benefit therefrom.
> The inadequacies of the District of Columbia Public School System, whether occasioned by insufficient funding or administrative inefficiency, certainly cannot be permitted to bear more heavily on the 'exceptional' or handicapped child than on the normal child.

The Court ordered the District to offer educational facilities within 30 days and required the School Board to develop a written plan for special education services and to identify those children within 45 days.

The following less known, but equally important, right to education lawsuits concern not only mentally retarded persons, but all handicapped children in their pursuit of an appropriate education. These lawsuits stress the responsibility of the state to allocate funds equitably and provide special educational services to all handicapped children.

In 1969, a decision by Judge D. Frank Wilkens, Third Judicial District Court of Utah, handed down a decision which required that two trainable mentally retarded children who had been excluded from education be provided an education within the public education system (*Wolf* v. *Legislature of State of Utah,* Note 3). Judge Wilkens noted:

> Today it is doubtful that any child may reasonably be expected to succeed in life if he is denied the right and opportunity of an education. In the instant case the segregation of the plaintiff children from the public school system has a detrimental effect upon the children as well as their parents. The impact is greater when it has the apparent sanction of the law. The policy of placing these children under the Department of Welfare and segregating them from the educational system can be and probably is usually interpreted as denoting their inferiority, unusualness, and incompetency. A sense of inferiority and not belonging affects the motivation of a child to learn. Segregation, even though perhaps well intentioned, under the apparent sanction of law and state authority has a tendency to retard the educational, emotional, and mental development of the children (*Wolf* v. *Legislature of the State of Utah,* Note 3).

Doe v. *Board of School Directors of the City of Milwaukee* (Note 4) was one of two suits filed in Wisconsin in 1970. In this class action suit the plaintiffs were represented by John Doe, a 14 year old trainable mentally retarded student. John Doe had been tested by a school board psychologist who determined him as eligible for placement in a class for the trainable mentally retarded. He was placed on a waiting list and the plaintiffs alleged that this was a violation of the equal protection clause of the Fourteenth Amendment of the United States Constitution. A temporary injunction was ordered and the public schools were prohibited from placing trainable mentally retarded children on a waiting list for special education. It also required the public schools to admit the plaintiffs into the program for trainable mentally retarded children with reasonable speed, which was 15 days.

Marlega v. *Milwaukee Board of School Directors* (Note 5) was a class action suit with Douglas Marlega as the plaintiff. He was excluded from public school attendance because of medical reasons involving hyperactivity without affording the parents or guardians an opportunity to contest the validity of the exclusion determination. A temporary restraining order was awarded on January 14, 1970, and on March 16, 1970, the Court ordered that no child could be excluded from a free public education on a full time basis without a due process hearing. This due process hearing includes (a) specification of the reasons for exclusion; (b) a prior hearing; (c) the rights to be represented by counsel, to confront and cross-examine witnesses, and to present evidence and witnesses on the child's behalf; (d) a stenographic record of the hearing; (e) a final decision in writing stating in detail the reasons for any exclusion; and (f) a specification of available public education alternatives (Cohen and DeYoung, 1973).

One right to education case, *Reid* v. *New York Board of Education* (Note 6), was decided in favor of the defendants due to the decision that a state court could provide an adequate remedy, and a decision by the Federal courts was unnecessary. A subsequent decision has not been made in this case brought before the state of New York in *Reid* v. *Board of Education* (Note 7). This class action suit was brought in Federal court to prevent the New York Board of Education from denying brain-injured children an appropriate education. It was alleged that over 400 children in New York City, identified as brain damaged, had not received placement because of a final screening procedure with an additional 200 children placed on a waiting list. In the new complaint the petitioner represented nine school age children with learning disabilities attributed to brain injury and/or emotional disturbance and they represented a class estimated to be 20,000 children. The children ranged in ages seven to 12 and had varied school histories which included misplacement, medical suspensions, home instruction, and assignments to waiting lists. The petition sought diagnosis and evaluation of all handicapped children and provision of complete educational services to this class of children. The decision is still pending before the New York Commissioner of Education.

The plaintiffs in *McMillan* v. *Board of Education of State of New York* (Note 8) were brain-injured children. They sought an injunction prohibiting a $2,000 ceiling on state payments for children in private schools and in addition included a request for provision of special classes in the public schools. Cohen and DeYoung (1973) report that the technique of waiting lists "insures non-attendance of the children, cools off the parent with the hope of eventual placement, and leaves the impression that the schools are doing something" (p. 274). A similar petition was charged in Massachusetts, in *Barnett* v. *Greenblatt* (Note 9), where 1,371 emotionally disturbed children were placed on a waiting list. This case, which is still pending, challenged the manner in which emotionally disturbed are arbitrarily denied the right to an education.

In Maryland, a class action suit was brought by the Maryland Association for Retarded Children and 14 mentally retarded children against the state of Maryland for failure to provide retarded or other handicapped children with an equal and free public education. It argued that the opportunity of an education, where the state has undertaken to provide it, is a right that must be made available to all on equal terms (*Maryland Association for Retarded Children* v. *State of Maryland,* Note 10).

Another class action suit was introduced on May 18, 1972, on behalf of 13 severely and moderately mentally retarded children in North Carolina for failure to provide "public education for all of the state's estimated 75,000 mentally retarded children." The defendants were the state, the state superintendent of public education, the state board of education, the department and the secretary of the department of human resources, and other officials of the state. The plaintiffs' attorneys used the North Carolina Constitution and a 1967 North Carolina attorney general's opinion as evidence that equal educational opportunities should be provided for all students. On July 31, 1972, the complaint was expanded to include in addition to the North Carolina Association for Retarded Children, 22 plaintiff children who

have by the defendants been denied the right to a free homebound instruction or been denied the right of tuition or costs reimbursement in private schools or institutions or been denied the right of free education, training or habilitation in institutions for mentally retarded (*North Carolina Association for Retarded Children, Inc.* v. *The State of North Carolina,* Note 11).

Another case was filed in the state of North Carolina on May 5, 1972, on behalf of all school age mentally retarded children in North Carolina (*Hamilton* v. *Riddle,* Note 12). Crystal Rene Hamilton, an eight year old mentally retarded child, was admitted to the Western Carolina Center, a state institution for the mentally retarded, in November, 1971, on a temporary basis. The center notified her parents after six months that they would no longer provide education and treatment for the child. The statutes of North Carolina were said to "guarantee equal free educational opportunities for all children of the state between the ages of six and twenty-one years of age." The case was joined with *North Carolina Association for Retarded Children, Inc.* v. *The State of North Carolina* (Note 11), and a decision has not been reached.

The coalition for the Civil Rights of Handicapped Persons and 12 handicapped children filed suit against the State of Michigan for their failure to provide a publicly supported education (*Harrison* v. *State of Michigan,* Note 13). The plaintiffs included many handicapping conditions—brain damage, mild to severe mental retardation, autism, emotional disturbance, cerebral palsy, and hearing disorders said to represent 30,000 to 40,000 handicapped children. The important difference in this suit was the reference in the complaint to a mandatory special education law effective July 1, 1972.

On October 30, 1972, United States District Judge Charles W. Joiner issued an order that dismissed the plaintiff's complaint. This was done on the basis that the new state of Michigan mandatory legislation rendered the complaint moot. He rendered an opinion that provision of education for some children while not providing it for others was a denial of equal protection, but that a comprehensive plan for the education of handicapped children could not be resolved by a judicial order.

A case which is still pending in Wisconsin was brought against the state by Mindy Linda Panitch representing a class of children "who are multi-handicapped, educable children between the ages of four and 20 years" (*Panitch* v. *State of Wisconsin,* Note 14). The outcome was a Wisconsin statute that enabled handicapped children to attend a special school, class or center, outside the state and required the county or school district to pay tuition and transportation to a public institution.

As a result of exclusion clauses in state statutes, a number of handicapped children have been denied an education. The course of action taken by attorneys has been to prove these statutes illegal. *Lori Case* v. *State of California* (Note 15) is an example of this particular strategy. Lori Case was a school age child diagnosed as autistic, deaf, and possibly mentally retarded who was enrolled in the multi-handicapped unit at the California School for the Deaf at Riverside, California, in May, 1970. After termination of her placement on grounds that she was severely mentally retarded and required custodial care beyond the provisions available at the school, the plaintiff filed and was granted a permanent injunction prohibiting defendants from interfering with Lori's placement. The question as in other right to education cases was centered around Lori's educability and the court's definition of the term. The plaintiff's attorney argued:

> There is absolutely no distinction in law, or in logic between a handicapped child and a physically normal child. Each is fully entitled to the equal protection and benefits of the laws of this State. Thus, to deprive Lori of her right to an education . . . would violate her fundamental rights (*Lori Case* v. *State of California,* Note 15).

The decision is still pending.

A similar case brought in California is *Burnstein* v. *The Board of Education* (Note 16) in which the plaintiffs were described as autistic and were not receiving a public education. It was argued that "education for children between the ages of six and 16 is not a mere privilege but is a legally enforceable right" under the state laws of California and the United States.

Another class of autistic children filed suit in August, 1972, against the state of Virginia for their legal right to be provided with equal access to an education. In addition to the use of the "fundamental rights" violation, the plaintiffs in *Tidewater Association for Autistic Children* v. *Commonwealth of Virginia* (Note 17) charged that discrimination was being practiced against autistic children "since they are educable and no suitable program of training or education is available for them." In December, 1972, the court dismissed the plaintiff's complaint on the grounds that the United States Constitution does not "explicitly or implicitly guarantee the right to a free public education." The court also explained that this right was guaranteed through the state laws of Virginia which called for the education of the handicapped. This was in some respect a defeat since no actual redress was accomplished.

The threat of money damages, as in other professional malpractice suits, might have been the forerunner of successful action in the following suits. In *Kivell* v. *Nemoitin* (Note 18), Fairfield County, Connecticut, the Superior Court ordered the board of education to pay $13,000 in back tuition costs to the mother of Seith Kivell, "a perceptually handicapped child with learning disabilities" to pay for two years of private education. In the ruling the judge, in anticipation of similar suits being brought, noted:

> This court will frown upon any unilateral action by parents in sending their children to other facilities, if a program is filed by a local board of education and is accepted and approved by the state board of education. Then it is the duty of the parents to accept the program . . . a refusal by parents in such a situation will not entitle their child to any benefits from this court (*Kivell* v. *Nemoitin,* Note 18).

A case held in New York Family Court awarded the cost of "private school education to be paid by the state." Peter Held had been enrolled in public schools for five years, three of which were in special education classes where his reading level never exceeded first grade level. After one year in private school, his reading level increased two grade levels. The mother had previously applied for funds under the same statutory provision but was denied. The court ruling in November, 1971, stated:

> It seems that now, for the first time in his young life, he has a future. This Court has the statutory duty to afford him an opportunity to achieve an education (*IN RE HELD,* Note 19).

A class action suit was filed in late 1972 in North Dakota on behalf of 13 retarded and handicapped children ages six to 19. Some of these children attended private schools, paid for by their parents, or lived in foster homes in a county where special education was available. Others received no education, attended private day care programs, or resided in state schools where no educational program was provided. The complaint alleged that only about 27 percent of the 25,000 exceptional children in North Dakota were receiving special services (*North Dakota Association for Retarded Children* v. *Peterson,* Note 20).

Another suit filed in December, 1972, named 19 physically and mentally handicapped children as plaintiffs in a class action suit against the state of Colorado for failure to provide equal educational opportunities to 20,000 handicapped children (*Colorado Association for Retarded Children* v. *State of Colorado,* Note 21).

RIGHT TO PLACEMENT

There is an increasing amount of litigation questioning the placement of children in special education on the basis of evaluative instruments that are considered prejudicial to the children on the basis of native language, cultural background, and normative standardization (Weintraub and Abeson, 1972). Much of the defense in these cases is based on the *Hobson* v. *Hansen* (Note 22) decision. This was the first time the use of testing to place and label children was questioned in court. The Washington, D. C. school system tracked children into four groups on the basis of test scores. Judge Skelly Wright ruled that the tracking system was illegal and in considering the evaluative measures used in the District he noted in *Hobson* (Note 22).

> Evidence shows that the method by which track assignments are made depends essentially on standardized aptitude tests which, although given on a system-wide basis, are completely inappropriate for use with a large segment of the student body. Because these tests are standardized primarily on and are relevant to a white middle class group of students, they produce inaccurate and misleading tests scores when given to lower class and Negro students. As a result rather than

> being classified according to ability to learn, these students are in reality being classified according to their socio-economic or racial status, or—more precisely—according to environmental and psychological factors which have nothing to do with innate ability.

He ordered the abolishment of the tracking system contending that it discriminated against the racially or economically disadvantaged and that it was in violation of the United States Constitution.

Another case where tracking or ability grouping was challenged was filed in the District Court of Southern California (*Spangler* v. *Board of Education,* Note 23). A group of black students charged that a racial imbalance existed because of the use of intelligence tests. The practice was halted due to the questionable validity of the tests, and the decision was made without contest.

In January, 1970, a suit was filed on behalf of nine Mexican-American public school students, aged eight through 13, who claimed they had been improperly placed in special education classes for the mentally retarded on the basis of inaccurate test scores (*Diana* v. *Board of Education,* Note 24). The children were from Spanish-speaking homes and when retested in Spanish, seven of the nine scored higher than the I.Q. qualification score for mental retardation. The case was settled out of court in favor of the plaintiffs. The final order required that:

1. Children are to be tested in their primary language. Interpreters may be used when a bilingual examiner is not available.
2. Mexican-American and Chinese children in classes for the educable mentally retarded are to be retested and evaluated.
3. The state will undertake immediate efforts to develop and standardize an appropriate I.Q. test.
4. Special efforts are to be extended to aid misplaced children readjust to regular classroom.

As a result of *Diana,* (Note 24), the United States Department of Health, Education and Welfare's office for Civil Rights issued a memorandum that informed the districts that they would be in violation of Title VI of the *Civil Rights Act* if students whose predominant language was other than English were assigned to classes for the mentally retarded on the basis of tests which evaluated the use of English language skills (Weintraub and Abeson, 1972).

Another related case, *Arreola* v. *Board of Education* (Note 25), questioned the placement of Mexican-American in special education classes and has not been settled.

In February, 1971, *Covarrubias* v. *San Diego Unified School District* (Note 26) was filed on behlf of 12 black and five Mexican-American pupils in classes for the mentally retarded. The plaintiffs relied on the attack used in *Dianas,* (Note 24) on the measuring instruments used for placement, the Stanford-Binet and Wechsler intelligence tests. The suit stated that many minority students were subjected to "taunts and derisions" because of a "biased testing procedure that does not recognize unfamiliarity with white, middle-class cultural background and a lack of facility was English." *Covarrubias* (Note 26) although similar to *Diana*, (Note 24), requested that revised tests be used that recognized the influence of the black ghetto. Money damages were asked to alleviate the wrong done to the children.

The *Stewart* v. *Phillips* (Note 27) case in Boston argued that the improper placement of poor or black students abridged the rights to equal protection and due process. The three classes of plaintiffs named were all poor or black Boston public school students, improperly placed, denied placement, and all parents of students placed in special classes but denied participation in the placement. The plaintiffs sought $20,000 in compensatory and punitive damages. *Stewart* (Note 27) went further than *Covarrubias* (Note 26) when it asked that I.Q. tests recognize the black culture and the influence that poverty has had on educational potential. A final decision has not been made, but Massachusetts school officials have developed new state regulations for special class placement.

Another placement issue was tested in Arizona which involved the disproportionate number of bilingual children enrolled in classes for the mentally handicapped. This suit, *Guadalupe Organization, Inc.* v. *Tempe Elementary School District* (Note 28), was filed by Mexican-American and Yaqui Indian school children. The complaint asked that children in classes for the retarded be reassessed, and that the "defendants be enjoined from administering tests to students who may do poorly on them because of their cultural background," and that no child be placed before the age of 10. A stipulated agreement provided for the consideration of cultural background, intelligence tests administered in the child's primary language, the parents' involvement in the placement, and the school's justification for any proportion of an ethnic group which is significantly greater than that group in the total school population.

In *Larry P.* v. *Riles* (Note 29), the plaintiffs were six black elementary school students from San Francisco Unified School District who represented a class of black children who alleged that they were inappropriately classified and placed in classes for the mentally retarded. The complaint held that this misplacement carried a stigma and "a life sentence of illiteracy and public dependency." Statistical information indicated that a disproportionate number were enrolled in classes for the retarded, and the plaintiffs were retested by black psychologists who obtained I.Q. scores which ranged from 79 to 104 and were above the retarded level (Cohen and DeYoung, 1973, p. 270). On June 20, 1972, the court ruled:

> . . . no black student may (in the future) be placed in an EMR class on the basis of criteria which rely primarily on the results of I.Q. tests as they are currently administered if the consequence of use of such criteria is racial imbalance in the composition of EMR classes (*Larry P.*, Note 29, p. 2033).

Eight black children classified as mentally retarded brought suit against New Orleans Parish School Board on the basis that the classification was done "arbitrarily and without standards or valid reasons" (*Lebanks* v. *Spears*, Note 30). It was also charged that the defendants failed to provide educational opportunities to some retarded children. The plaintiffs' attorneys stated:

> Continued deprivation (of education) will render each plaintiff and member of the class functionally useless in our society; each day leaves them further behind their more fortunate peers.

In addition to appropriate classification procedures, they sought a $20,000 damage aware for each plaintiff. A decision has not been reached.

In *Ruiz* v. *State Board of Education* (Note 31) three Mexican-American children filed a class action suit against the state of California opposing the use of I.Q.'s in their educational evaluation. The action sought relief in the form of prevention of the placement of group I.Q.'s in school records. An injunction was sought to prevent the use of group intelligence tests in the determination of allocation of funds.

Walton v. *City School District of Glen Cove* (Note 32) concerned Lynn Walton, a 15 year old, who was suspended from regular school attendance for "verbally abusing a teacher and refusing to follow her directions." It was alleged that the label "handicapped" or "emotionally disturbed" was arbitrarily assigned, and that it resulted in Lynn Walton being stigmatized as inferior and unfit. On February 4, 1972, the court granted the relief sought by the petitioner recognizing the school district's violation of procedural due process.

The cases presented here are but the tip of an iceberg which increasingly threatens the current practice of school psychology. Quite clearly, there is considerable need for careful attention to the expectations of the courts placed upon education. School psychologists cannot afford to be uninformed and unimpressed.

REFERENCE NOTES

1. *Pennsylvania Association for Retarded Children* v. *Commonwealth of Pennsylvania,* Civil Action No. 71–42 (E. D. Pa. 1971).
2. *Mills* v. *Board of Education of the District of Columbia,* Civil Action No. 1939–71 (Dist. of Columbia, 1971).
3. *Wolf* v. *Legislature of the State of Utah,* Civil Action No. 182646 (3d Judicial Dist. Ct. Utah 1969).
4. *Doe* v. *Board of School Directors of the City of Milwaukee,* (U. S. District Ct., E. D. Wis., 1970).
5. *Marlega* v. *Board of School Directors of the City of Milwaukee,* Civil Action No. 70-C-8 (E. D. Wis. 1970).
6. *Reid* v. *New York Board of Education,* Civil Action No. 71–1380 (U. S. Dist. Ct., S.D.N.Y. 1971).
7. *Reid* v. *Board of Education,* Administrative Procedure Before the State Commissioner of Education, 1972.
8. *McMillan* V. *Board of Education of State of New York,* 430 F. 2d. 1145 (2d Cir. 1970).
9. *Barnett* v. *Greenblatt* (U. S. District Ct. 1971).
10. *Maryland Association for Retarded Children* v. *State of Maryland,* Civil Action No. 72-733-K (U. S. Dist. Ct., Md. 1972).
11. *North Carolina Association for Retarded Children, Inc.* v. *The State of North Carolina,* Civil Action No. 72–72 (U. S. Dist. Ct. N. C., Raleigh Div. 1972).
12. *Hamilton* v. *Riddle,* Civil Action No. 72–86 (U. S. District Ct., W. D. of N. C., Charlotte Div. 1972).
13. *Harrison* v. *State of Michigan,* Civil Action No. 38357 (U. S. District Ct., E. D. Mich. S. D. 1972).
14. *Panitch* v. *State of Wisconsin,* Civil Action No. 72-L-461 (U. S. Dist. Ct., Wis. 1972).
15. *Lori Case* v. *State of California,* Civil Action No. 101679 (Cal. Superior Ct., Riverside City, Cal. 1972).

16. *Burnstein* v. *The Board of Education* (California S. Ct., Contra Costa City. 1970).
17. *Tidewater Association for Autistic Children* v. *Commonwealth of Virginia,* Civil Action No. 426-72-N, (U. S. Dist. Ct., E. D. Va. 1972).
18. *Kivell* v. *Nemoitin,* No. 143913, (Sup. Ct., Fairfield Cty., Conn. 1972).
19. *IN RE HELD,* Docket Nos. H-2-71 and H-10-71, (N. Y. Family Ct., Westchester Cty., N. Y. 1971).
20. *North Dakota Association for Retarded Children* v. *Peterson,* (U. S. Dist. Ct., N. Dakota 1972).
21. *Colorado Association for Retarded Children* v. *State of Colorado,* (U. S. District Ct., Col. 1972).
22. *Hobsons v. Hansen* - II, 320 F. Supp. 720 (D. D. C. 1971).
23. *Spangler* v. *Board of Education,* 311 F. Supp. 501 (S. D. Cal. 1970).
24. *Diana* v. *Board of Education,* Civil Action No. C-70-37 (N. D. Cal. 1970).
25. *Arreola* v. *Board of Education,* Case No. 160–577 (Superior Ct., Orange Cty., Cal. 1968).
26. *Covarrubias* v. *San Diego Unified School District,* Civil Action No. 70–30d (S. D. Cal. 1971).
27. *Stewart* v. *Phillips,* Civil Action No. 70–1199 F (D. Mass. 1970).
28. *Guadalupe* v. *Tempe Elementary School District,* Stipulation and Order (January 24, 1972).
29. *Larry P.* v. *Riles,* 41 U. S. L. W. 2033 (U. S. June 21, 1972).
30. *Lebanks* v. *Spears,* Civil Action No. 71 2897 (U. S. Dist. Ct., E. D. Louisiana, New Orleans Div. 1971).
31. *Ruiz* v. *State Board of Education,* Civil Action No. 218294 (Superior Ct. Cal. 1971).
32. *Walton* v. *City School District of Glen Cove,* Index No. 18209–71 (Supreme Ct. N. Y. 1972).

REFERENCES

Cohen, J., & DeYoung, H. The role of litigation in the improvement of programming for the handicapped. In L. Mann and D. Sabatino (Eds.) *The first review of special education.* Philadelphia, Pa.: Buttonwood Farms, Inc., 1973, 261–284.

Gilhool, T. K. The uses of litigation: the right of retarded children to a free public education. *Peabody Journal of Education,* 1973, *50,* 120–128. (a)

Mental Health Law Project. *Basic rights of the mentally handicapped.* Washington, D. C.: Author, 1973.

Weintraub, F. and Abeson, A. Appropriate education for all handicapped children: a growing issue. *Syracuse Law Review,* 1972, *23,* 1037–1058.

R. Kaye Theimer
Tulsa, Oklahoma

Omer J. Rupiper
Professor of Education
The University of Oklahoma
820 Van Vleet Oval
Norman, Oklahoma 73069

Journal of School Psychology
1975 • Vol. 13, No. 4

LAW, EDUCATIONAL REFORM, AND THE SCHOOL PSYCHOLOGIST

PETER KURILOFF
University of Pennsylvania

Summary: The law has become a major vehicle for those seeking to reform education. The two areas of reform which most affect school psychologists are the extension of the right to a public education to previously discriminated against and excluded groups, and the extension of the protection of the Bill of Rights to all school children. The potential impact of these areas on the role of the school psychologist is suggested by preliminary findings on one such reform, the right of retarded children to an appropriate education and the guarantee of that right through the provision of procedural due process. Any response to the reform by school psychologists will involve risks and opportunities which must be carefully weighed if a wise choice is to be made from the point of view of both children and the profession.

When the Supreme Court ruled in *Brown v. Board of Education* (Note 1) that "Today, education is perhaps the most important function of the state and local governments . . . [and] where the state has undertaken to provide it, [it] is a *right* which must be available to all on equal terms," (p. 493) it did more than end legal segregation in public schools. It raised the hopes of all minority groups and opened the way for a veritable flood of suits. The most important of these concern two areas: the access of various kinds of children to equal education opportunity and, perhaps less directly, the extension to all children of the protection of the Bill of Rights.

After *Brown*, in which the court found that separate facilities were not and could not be equal, several key cases attacked many of the central organizational features of schools. Shortly after the Washington, D.C., schools ended their segregated system, they instituted a tracking system. Soon, black and poor children were vastly overrepresented in the lowest track. Federal Judge J. Skelley Wright saw no evil motive in this, yet he ruled in *Hobson v. Hansen* (Note 2) that it constituted an invidious discrimination which, while arising from ". . . an arbitrary quality of thoughtlessness . . ." was nevertheless " . . . as disastrous and unfair to private rights and the public interest as the perversity of a willful scheme." (p. 513) He also criticized the de facto segregation of both students and faculty and the disparity in resources available to predominantly white versus black schools. In a second *Hobson* decision, he ordered that both human and material resources be equalized across the district (*Hobson v. Hansen*, Note 3).

Almost simultaneous to the second *Hobson* (1971) suit, the Pennsylvania Association for Retarded Children (PARC) sought to extend the right to

An earlier version of this paper was presented to the Annual School Psychology Conference, Pennsylvania State University, October 23, 1974.

education to all retarded children. After a day of testimony in which the accumulated weight of much research evidence created a convincing argument that no child is ineducable, that behavior modification techniques make even the most severely retarded child accessible to some improvement, that retarded children tend to serious regression when out of a program for even a little while, and finally, that many children in EMR classes are misclassified, the State agreed to settle the case (*Pennsylvania Association for Retarded Children v. The Commonwealth of Pennsylvania*, Note 4).

While the parties settled without the Court ruling on the constitutional merits of the case, the *PARC* decree nevertheless was a landmark which has since generated suits and reform legislation across the nation. Besides requiring the state to find and include all retarded children in an appropriate program within the presumption that the closer to normal a program is the better, the decree recognized that the process of classification itself could result in serious harm to children and therefore sought to protect them through mandatory periodic review, yearly review at parental request, and for those parents dissatisfied with their child's placement, an impartial due process hearing. While the requirements of procedural due process vary, depending on the context in which it is found (Buss, 1971) in the *PARC* case it meant that parents were entitled to adequate notice of a placement decision and that they had the right to examine their child's records, the right to counsel, the right to call and cross-examine witnesses, and the opportunity to appeal unfavorable decisions for cause.

The *PARC* suit soon was followed by *Mills v. the Board of Education* (Note 5). Through it the plaintiffs sought to establish the principle that *all* children, from the blind to the incorrigibly disruptive—regardless of their exceptionality—were constitutionally entitled to a free public education. Judge Joseph Waddy concurred, finding constitutional warrant for the universal right to education in both *Brown* (1954) and *Hobson* (1967). He concluded that "due process of law requires a hearing prior to exclusion, termination, or classification into a special program" (*Mills*, Note 5, p. 875).

A variety of other recent suits have begun to attack subtler school practices than those addressed in *PARC* and *Mills*. In *Larry P. v. Riles* (Note 6) the plaintiff noted that the percentage of blacks in EMR classes was twice that of whites and argued that the assignment process itself was at fault. The court ordered an end to the use of paper and pencil IQ tests to classify children. When the percentage of blacks increased after the decision, the plaintiffs went back to court, asking it to place a moratorium on all testing until either a reasonable quota system for EMR placement or a culture-fair assessment instrument could be developed. Similarly, in *Diana v. State Board of Education* (Note 7) the court ordered an end to the assignment of chicano children to EMR classes simply because they are not fluent in English. Now school psychologists in California must use a Spanish form of the WISC when testing chicanos, while all districts must develop plans to end racial imbalance in special education.

A final group of cases has just begun to emerge. In these, representatives of various minority groups, such as Chinese (*Lau v. Nichols*, Note 8) and chicano Americans (*Serna v. Portales Municipal Schools*, Note 9), have asked courts to require schools to account in their curriculum for real differences in backgrounds—and they have begun to win. It is no longer enough for schools to offer a general program geared to the dominant white cultural norm (Katz, 1972) if some of their students cannot take advantage of it (Kirp, 1974).

In summary then, legal reform of education having to do with equal opportunity began by outlawing segregation by race, then turned to exclusion for exceptionality, and now is beginning to focus on the very heart of the educational enterprise—the curriculum itself. Courts have had a similar impact on the way in which school officials may construe their role as moral educators of the young.

Since the early nineteenth century and before, the traditional view of the courts has been that educators should have a wide degree of latitude in regulating the behavior of their students. They reasoned that educators could use their professional judgment to impose punishments or controls as long as these were rationally related to the legitimate end of inculcating discipline and respect for authority (Mandel, 1974). Since the middle 1940's a more modern view has begun to prevail. This view holds that whenever students' behavior falls within activity protected by the Constitution, school officials may neither control nor punish them for it. Only when there is no other way to prevent infringement on the rights of others, or material and substantial disruption of the order necessary to maintain the operation of the school, may they discipline students for exercising their constitutional rights. Even here, the courts place the burden on the school district to prove students' behavior is dangerous or disruptive to the orderly business of the school (Buss, 1971; Mandel, 1974). Many of the key cases require due process hearings prior to the school's taking any action which might result either in serious harm—such as dismissal—to the children involved or in a restriction of their constitutional rights (*Dixon v. Alabama,* Note 10; *Woods v. Wright*, Note 11; *Goss v. Lopez*, Note 12).

Once again we see in realm of students' rights, as well as in the area of equal educational opportunity, a trend toward the inclusion of children, the expansion of their constitutional rights, and the creation of quasi-legal procedures to protect them.

IMPACT ON THE SCHOOL PSYCHOLOGIST

What have these rulings done to the role of the school psychologist? As the persons responsible under the law in most states for the evaluation of special children, we have automatically become the ones responsible for the classification decisions. There is no way we can pass the buck to superiors; we are in the role precisely because we have the professional knowledge others—often our putative superiors—do not have (McDermott, 1972). This authority of knowledge renders us theoretically liable for any damages we cause children through a misapplication of our powers. While school psychologists are usually not primary defendants in a suit, that honor being reserved for school boards and superintendents, there is at least one case in which plaintiffs requested compensatory and punitive damages for the purportedly misclassified children involved (*Stewart v. Phillips*, Note 13).[1]

[1] To the best of my knowledge, this case was negotiated out of court and thus the issue of the school psychologist's liability in cases of misclassification was never decided.

A much more realistic assumption is that we will be called upon to testify in due process hearings more and more frequently. Here, publicly, we will be asked to present our qualifications, justify our methods, and defend our decisions. What is more, we will be confronted with situations in which our easy assumption that we are "all looking to find what is best for Johnny" will be questioned by Johnny's lawyer, who, more often than not, will view us as "hostile." Perhaps more important, whether or not we must actually be a witness at a hearing, wisdom requires that we treat every case as if it were a real possibility. Furthermore, if Pennsylvania is an example, we will be confronted with all of this under the pressure of a great deal more work – work demanded of us both by the increased number of pupils under our jurisdiction and the increased demand for evaluations and re-evaluations.[2] How have school psychologists in Pennsylvania responded to this challenge to date?

The Project on Student Classification and the Law[3] is seeking answers to such questions through an extensive evaluation of the impact of the landmark *PARC* agreement. Preliminary case studies[4] have examined impact as a function of the degree of a school district's urbanization, the complexity of its organizational structure, and the degree to which its school psychologists identify with its purposes, as well as with those of the particular children they are called upon to help. Pennsylvania's 569 school districts are grouped into 29 Intermediate Units (I.Us.) which disburse state revenues and provide resources and services, including much of the state's special education, that many individual districts otherwise could not afford. For our pilot studies we chose one urban and one rural I.U. and did extensive interviews with all the key special education administrative personnel at both the I.U. and district level. We also interviewed principals, guidance counselors, social workers, and teachers. What did we discover in each area?

In the urban I.U. school psychologists found themselves within a highly structured, formal bureaucratic setting in which decision making was fully centralized. People operated by carefully delineated rules and procedures.

[2] A conservative estimate suggests that each Pennsylvania school psychologist spends approximately 152 hours more per year on assessments than he did prior to *PARC.* This figure was arrived at as follows: Before the *PARC* agreement, there were aproximately 51,000 retarded children in public school in Pennsylvania. These children had to be re-evaluated every three years by state statute. Assuming a relatively stable population of retarded children, this meant psychologists had approximately 17,000 evaluations and re-evaluations to do every year. The suit added about 7,400 previously excluded children and about 2,600 new retarded children to the schools rolls. It also required that all children be re-evaluated at least every two years. This meant psychologists in the post *PARC* era had approximately 30,500 evaluations and re-evaluations to do annually. Interviews conducted by State Department of Education official Jerry Hearsum with a sample of the state's school psychologists indicate that approximately 4.5 hours are required to carry out each assessment. Thus, following *PARC*, $[(30{,}500-17{,}000) \times 4.5] \div 400$ or 151.875 hours per year were added to the average school psychologist's load.

[3] Research carried out by the Project on Student Classification and the Law is supported in part by National Institute of Education Grant No. NEG–00–3–0192. The opinions expressed herein do not necessarily reflect the position or policy of the National Institute of Education, and no official endorsement should be inferred.

[4] I want to gratefully acknowledge the assistance of Bruce Dworkin, Research Associate, and Jeffrey Young, Research Assistant, Project on Student Classification and the Law, who helped design these studies and who carried out the interviews during June and July, 1974.

The psychologists' roles were narrowly defined to include testing and evaluation. They applied a diagnostic label to children and wrote accompanying prescriptions without reference to any specific program within the district. When parents objected to a proposed placement, the psychologist usually had little or nothing to do with any ensuing negotiations between the parents and the district. Under these circumstances it was rare for the psychologists to know what actually happened to the children following assessment. Such follow-up was left to other professionals whose roles were equally constricted. Thus, the school psychologists within the urban setting we examined did almost no consultation, had almost no contact with programs, and almost never followed the children after they had been evaluated. Nevertheless, they enjoyed distant but cordial relationships with teachers and principals. While these school people sometimes complained about the psychologists' lack of accessibility and apparent inability to offer concrete suggestions regarding the management of individual children, they did see the psychologists as effective in helping them remove troublesome children and for this they were genuinely grateful.

In the rural setting psychologists found themselves in a loosely structured, informal organization in which decision making was decentralized and people tended to operate less by rules and regulations than by informal agreements. The role of the psychologists was broadly defined to encompass testing and evaluation, followed by consultation with special educators. This in turn led to actual assignment of children to specific programs. When parents objected to placements, a negotiation process ensued in which the school psychologists played a mediating role between school officials and the parents, even though they very well may have been the ones who originated the assignment. Most often such disagreements arose from the school's wish to remove children from a more normal to a less normal placement as defined by the Consent Agreement. The outcome of the negotiation process was a variety of placements, some ideal, some perhaps compromising the best interests of the children in the interest of resolving the conflicts.

Once the children were placed, the psychologists maintained responsibility for following their progress, making periodic reports on it, and generally keeping tabs on the wisdom of the initial placement decisions. In this setting the psychologists enjoyed close, often rocky relationships with teachers and principals. While the more open teachers often appreciated the psychologists' consultative help, some teachers and principals were angered by instances in which psychologists had refused to remove children from their schools. In one case a particularly outspoken psychologist, who had taken the side of a child's parents in a due process hearing, was told outright that her job would be in jeopardy if she didn't "work with the school district more closely."

We found then, that in the context of a highly centralized, formal urban school organization, school psychologists tended to define their role narrowly, as professionals certifying through testing the placement of children according to the letter of state statutes. This meant children's needs were fulfilled most often when they coincided with organizational demands and expectations. In the context of a decentralized, informal rural school organization, school psychologists tended to define their role broadly, as professionals seeking the most appropriate placement of children through testing, observation of current and proposed placements, consultations with teachers and parents, and follow-up evaluations of individuals and programs. This meant children's needs were usually fulfilled, even when they conflicted with organizational imperatives. Not surprisingly, psychologists in this setting tended to experience more conflict with other members of their organization than did those in the urban location.

IMPLICATION FOR THE FUTURE ROLE OF THE SCHOOL PSYCHOLOGIST

If these findings hold up—and, based on literature of role conflict and legal impact (Mandel, 1973; Dworkin, Note 14), we believe they will—school psychology stands at a peculiar, challenging, and dangerous juncture. We find ourselves caught between our sacred concern for the well-being of children and our duties to the organizations which employ us. We can respond by construing our role narrowly to meet the internal pressure and demands of the schools, or broadly, to meet both the external demands of the parents and children we serve and the needs of the schools. It might be argued that it is precisely to avoid organizational conflicts that many of us have already chosen a narrow role. Yet, if current legal realities mean anything, they mean that the choice of either role involves both risks and opportunities. In trying to make a decision under such circumstances, wisdom would dictate we take into account as many of the positive and negative consequences as possible.

Whose agents are we? Most of us will readily assert we are working for the child. Yet, forced into a quasi-judicial hearing, where will we stand? Probably as witnesses for the school in an adversary setting (Rice, 1961). Fortunately, most of our time will be taken up trying to find solutions to emergent problems long before they evolve into such serious conflicts. And here is where we can bring our power to bare. In what does that power lie?

Writing in an earlier issue of the *Journal of School Psychology*, Nadine Lambert (1973) traced the traditional sources of school psychologists' power and influence to their ability to accurately assess individual differences *and* both to identify special educational needs and develop appropriate programs for meeting them. Our specialized knowledge of individual and program assessment makes us the "official gatekeepers" for the system (Lewin, 1951). Backed by decisions like *PARC*, we have great and growing authority, whether we choose to exercise it or not, over who remains in what class or program and who is removed from what program or class. In large measure we can determine "in" and "out," "when" and "where." But such precedent-setting decisions also give us a growing authority over the entire realm of special education programs. In states where similar laws are promulgated—and the list of states is growing—we will be able to decide whether a program is "appropriate" or "suitable" to a particular child's needs, and presumably, when it stops being suitable. In effect, this gives us a veritable, albeit defacto, veto power over the form, content, and quality of special education. To be the only ones in the educational system who can make such decisions legally, is potentially very painful and very powerful. How can we use our growing control both wisely and well?

From the outset we must delicately balance the perceived needs of the school, and particularly the teacher—to take the example of a child who is in a regular class and whom the teacher wishes removed—with the real needs of the child. This is frought with risks. In such cases we often encounter unusual pressure from the teacher and the principal for removal. On the one hand, in the cases where assessment shows removal to be unwarranted, professional judgment and a growing body of law demand we require the child to remain. Yet can we do so without systematically helping the teacher to cope with the child? If we do not, we abandon both the child and the teacher and probably incur their anger as well. If we do try to help her, we will need to know how to be effective consultants—and we will need enough help ourselves to have the time to do it. On the other hand, in the cases where assessment reveals a child should be removed, professional judgment and the law demand we propose a genuinely appropriate alternative program. Can we do so without systematically evaluating the efficacy of the special education programs available to us? If we do not, we abandon the child to the kinds of uncertainties that lead to law suits, or worse, to the wasting of a human being. If we do, we will need to know how to carry out reliable and valid program evaluations—and we will need enough extra help to have the time to do it.

Of course I have only gone through one permutation of the possible decisions we are called upon to make daily. Depending on the kind of role we choose to play and the accuracy of our judgments, each decision entails its own opportunities and risks, its own potential for expanding the meaning and power of our role. Interviews carried out by the Project on Student Classification and the Law during the 1972–73 school year (Kirp, Buss & Kuriloff, 1974) and the Project's pilot data (Dworkin & Young, Note 15) suggest the most important of these risks and opportunities. Tables 1 & 2 summarize them as a function of the accuracy of the assessment decision and the breadth of the psychologist's role definition.

A glance at the tables is enough to show that a narrow role definition carries with it most of the risks and costs, and fewest, but by no means necessarily the least persuasive, of the opportunities and gains. When psychologists who have adopted it make correct placement decisions based on careful testing, they are minimizing the chances of a law suit or hearing, while meeting the organizational demands for adherence to statutory labeling criteria. If the decisions result in children's removal from regular to special classes, organizational demands for the removal of disturbing children are also satisfied, winning the psychologists the appreciation of people they depend on for support and fellowship. But, if the decisions are for maintaining children in regular classes, the likelihood grows that the psychologists will face increased hostility and pressure from frustrated teachers and parents.

Psychologists who define their role narrowly are in large measure protected from learning about such reactions by the insularity of their position within the formal organizational structure and by the statutory correctness of their decisions. This may in some measure compensate for these costs and, in part, account for the persistence of the role.

Table 1
Potential Opportunities and Gains Vs. Risks and Costs of Placement Decisions to Leave Children in Regular Class Made by School Psychologists Holding Narrow Vs. Broad Role Definitions

Role Definition	Correct Decisions	
	Opportunities and Gains	Risks and Costs
Narrow	Legally correct decision to leave child in regular class greatly decreases likelihood of suit or due process hearing. "Test and place" role enables psychologist to meet organizational demands for mandated labeling.	Since the child continues to disturb the teacher, pressures from the school on the psychologist to remove the child will remain. The teacher and principal are likely to be annoyed with the psychologist, thus limiting their acceptance of any help he may offer in the future. A disturbing child will have to cope with a frustrated teacher, possibly causing even more disturbance in the system of the school. The child's parents may pressure the school to do more for their child.
Broad	Legally correct decision to leave child in regular class greatly decreases likelihood of suit or due process hearing. The psychologist has the change to consult with the teacher about an issue the teacher considers important. If the psychologist helps the teacher help the child, he has begun to teach the teacher to help all such children. Enough successful consultation may foster preventive behavior on the part of the teacher and therefore lead to a lessening of demands to "test and place."	The district may pressure the psychologist to provide mandated scores for labeling, thus creating serious conflicts between organizational and professional loyalities.

Table 1 cont.

	Incorrect Decisions	
	Opportunities and Gains	Risks and Costs
Narrow	The chances the parents will initiate a suit or due process hearing are reduced.	Since the child continues to disturb the teacher, pressures from the school on the psychologist to remove the child will remain. The teacher and principal are likely to be annoyed with the psychologist, thus limiting their acceptance of any help he or she may offer in the future. A disturbing child will have to cope with a frustrated teacher, possibly causing even more disturbance in the system of the school. Should a suit or due process hearing be initiated, the psychologist may find himself in the embarrassing position of being contradicted in an open public forum.
Broad	Chances the parents will initiate a suit or due process hearing are reduced. The psychologist has the change to consult with the teacher about an issue the teacher considers important. While such consultation is more difficult when the child is improperly placed, if the psychologist helps the teacher help the child, he has begun to teach the teacher to help all such children. Enough successful consultation may foster preventive behavior on the part of the teacher and therefore lead to a lessening of demands to "test and place."	The district may pressure the psychologist to provide mandated scores for labeling, thus creating serious conflicts between organizational and professional loyalties. Should a suit or due process hearing be initiated, the psychologist may find himself in the embarrassing position of being contradicted in an open public forum.

Table 2
Potential Opportunities and Gains vs. Risks and Costs of Placement Decisions to Remove Children from Regular to Special Class of School Psychologists Holding Narrow Vs. Broad Role Definitions

Role Definition	Correct Decisions	
	Opportunities and Gains	Risks and Costs
Narrow	Organizational demands are satisfied by removal of the disturbing child.	If parents are sensitive to potential stigmatizing impact of special education, the psychologist and the school face the possibility of a suit or due process hearing. Since the psychologist does not either explore prior to placement or do a follow-up evaluation of child and program, the child is abandoned to the vagaries of the particular school system. If the child's experience is bad, the parents' dissatisfaction may cause them to initiate a suit or due process hearing.
Broad	Organizational demands are satisfied by removal of the disturbing child. The psychologist's exploration of the program prior to placement and follow-up evaluations of both child and program increase the likelihood the child will receive an appropriate education. The psychologist's contacts with the parents prior to placement and during follow-up reduce the likelihood of a suit or due process hearing.	While greatly reduced, there is still a possibility that the parents will initiate a suit or due process hearing.

Table 2 cont.

	Incorrect Decisions	
	Opportunities and Gains	Risks and Costs
Narrow	Organizational demands are satisfied by removal of the disturbing child.	The possibility of a parent initiated suit or due process hearing is maximized in these circumstances. The child will be unnecessarily stigmatized. The child may be retarded educationally by improper placement. Should a suit or due process hearing be initiated, the psychologist may find himself in the embarrassing position of being contradicted in an open public forum.
Broad	Organizational demands are satisfied by removal of the disturbing child. Because the psychologist contacts the parents prior to placement, explains the program, and does a follow-up evaluation of both the program and child, the possibility of the parents' initiating a suit or a due process hearing is diminished. The psychologist's exploration prior to placement and his follow-up afterward lessens the possibility the child will be retarded educationally.	The possibility of a suit, though diminished, remains. The child will be unnecessarily stigmatized. Should a suit or due process hearing be initiated, the psychologist may find himself in the embarrassing position of being contradicted in an open public forum.

Certainly psychologists who define their role broadly will find it almost impossible to avoid feedback about their performance. Correct decisions for removal will protect them as well as their narrowly defined colleagues, and also at once reduce the chance of parental misunderstandings and increase the likelihood that placement will prove genuinely beneficial to children. But correct decisions to leave children in regular classes, coupled with the constant school contact built into the broad role, will expose psychologists to the complaints and frustrations of the teachers and principals who originate the referrals. Of course this also presents the psychologists with key opportunities to consult with the affected school personnel. To the extent their consultation helps teachers overcome problems the teachers themselves define as important, the psychologists will increase both the appreciation of, and the demand for, their services. And to the extent the psychologists self-consciously communicate their approach to problems, they may actually succeed in "giving away" their skills, thus fostering preventive behavior on the part of the teachers with whom they work (Kuriloff, 1973). The intricacy of this process, the satisfaction of knowing how to do it well, and its multiplier effect when well done, probably account for the growing interest in the broad role, despite its inherent potential for generating conflict.

The balance sheet is much the same when the effects of incorrect placement decisions are examined. While psychologists run the greatest risk of a suit or due process hearing when they mistakenly remove children from regular to special classes, those with a narrow definition, because of their limited contact with parents and their lack of knowledge of placements, are likely to evoke the most negative reactions, and therefore, end up in court with situations that are often amicably resolved by their more broadly defined colleagues. This may be of little comfort to psychologists with broader role definitions. Although their continued follow-up of placed children at least gives them opportunities to recognize their mistakes, these psychologists are faced with the knowledge that such decisions must unnecessarily stigmatize wrongly labeled children. For the same reason, psychologists with a narrow role definition cannot take much pleasure in satisfying the school's needs through such decisions; generally, they will not even have the chance to correct them unless, of course, parents request a hearing!

When incorrect decisions to leave children in regular classes are made, the chances of a suit or due process hearing are reduced for both types of psychologists. Those with a narrow role definition may run more of a risk of conflict with teachers and principals than with any of the decisions they are likely to make, but again, they will be protected by their insularity within the organization. Those with a broader definition must deal with the consequences of both their errors and of leaving the children where they do not belong. Yet, once again, their ongoing consultation with teachers means they have the opportunity to provide extra support for teachers, to recognize their errors, and to rectify them.

CONCLUSIONS

Essentially the Project's data suggest that those of us who choose a narrow role may experience less tension-inducing encounters with our fellow educators than those of us who define our role more broadly, but we may only gain this tranquility at the cost of facing more law suits, due process hearings, and a job description that is so constricted it threatens to price us out of business. Already in at least one state top education officials have begun to toy with the idea of contracting out the psychological services they find so dear, as well as reforming legislation to allow psychometrists to carry the major burden of assessment. Those of us who choose an expanded role probably will experience more conflicts and tensions in our dealings with our colleagues in the schools, but we probably will have less difficulties with the courts. Our jobs will also be much more demanding than those of our narrowly defined colleagues. In order to perform competently, besides our traditional knowledge of individual differences and program evaluation, we will have to acquire consultation and program development skills. Our graduate training programs will have to be altered to educate future professionals in this new knowledge, but also to provide those of us already in the field with continuing education. And, finally, we will have to take an active part in strengthening our professional networks so the expanded role gains commensurate recognition in the power structure of the schools.

How will we choose to go? It is not clear. The opportunities which face us are at least as exciting as the risks they entail are frightening. We will make the most of them if we trust with Goethe that:

> When we treat ourselves as we are,
> We make ourselves worse than we are.
> When we treat ourselves as if we were already
> What we potentially could become,
> We begin to make ourselves what we can be.

1. *Brown v. Board of Education,* 347 U.S. 483, (1954).
2. *Hobson v. Hansen,* 629 F. Supp. 401 (D.D.C. 1967).
3. *Hobson v. Hansen,* 327 F. Supp. 844 (D.D.C. 1971).
4. *Pennsylvania Association for Retarded Children v. The Commonwealth of Pennsylvania,* 343 F. Supp. 279 (E.D.Pa. 1972).
5. *Mills v. Board of Education,* 348 F. Supp. 866 (D.D.C. 1972).
6. *Larry P. v. Riles,* 343 F. Supp. 1306 (N.D. Cal. 1972).
7. *Diana v. State Board of Education,* No. C-70–37 (N.D. Cal., 1970).
8. *Lau v. Nichols,* 483 F. 2d (9th Cir. 1973), Cert, granted, 412 US938 (1973).
9. *Serna v. Portales Municipal Schools,* 351 F. Supp. 1279 (D.N.M. 1972).
10. *Dixon v. Alabama Board of Education,* 294 F.2nd 150 (5th Cir. 1961).
11. *Woods v. Wright,* 334 F. 2d 369 (5th Cir. 1964).
12. *Goss v. Lopez,* 43 *U.S. Law Week,* 4181, 1/22/75.
13. *Stewart v. Phillips,* 70–1199–F. (D.Mass. 1970).
14. Dworkin, B. *Reference group orientation of professionals and role definition in open educational bureaucracies.* Unpublished manuscript prepared for the Project on Student Classification and the Law, University of Pennsylvania, 1974.
15. Dworkin, B., & Young, J. *A proposal to study the organizational impact of legal reform on special education services in Pennsylvania.* Unpublished manuscript prepared for the Project on Student Classification and the Law, University of Pennsylvania, 1974.

REFERENCES

Buss, W. Procedural due process for school discipline: Probing the constitutional outline. *University of Pennsylvania Law Review*, 1971, 119, 545–641.

Katz, M. B. *Class, bureaucracy, and schools*. New York: Praeger Press, 1972.

Kirp, D., Buss, W., & Kuriloff, P. Legal reform of special education: Empirical studies and procedural proposals. *California Law Review*, 1974, *62*, 40–155.

Kuriloff, P. The counselor as psycho-ecologist. *American Personnel and Guidance Journal*, 1973, *51*, 321–327.

Lambert, N. M. The school psychologist as a source of influence and power. *Journal of School Psychology*, 1973, *11*, 245–250.

Lewin, K. *Field theory in social science*. New York: Harper Brothers, 1951.

Mandel, R. Judicial decisions and organizational change in public schools. *School Review*, 1974, *82*, 327–346.

McDermott, P. A. Law, liability, and the school psychologist: Malpractice and liability. *Journal of School Psychology*, 1972, *10*, 397–407.

Rice, G. P. The psychologist as expert witness. *American Psychologist*, 1961, *16*, 691–692.

Peter Kuriloff
Associate Professor
Graduate School of Education
University of Pennsylvania
3700 Walnut Street
Philadelphia, Pennsylvania 19174

Journal of School Psychology
1975 • Vol. 13, No. 4

LAW, PROFESSIONAL PRACTICE, AND PROFESSIONAL ORGANIZATIONS: WHERE DO WE GO FROM HERE?

VIRGINIA C. BENNETT JACK I. BARDON

Rutgers University

Summary: The ethical dilemmas presented to the practicing school psychologist by the plethora of laws that dictate procedures, policies, and instrumentation are discussed. The function of professional organizations, both national and state, is described as (a) anticipating legislation, (b) developing political impact, (c) affecting existing laws, and (d) affecting proposed legislation. Coordination of efforts among various groups and development of political expertise is urged as a way to approach issues of concern to both psychologists and their clients.

As professional practitioners we consider ourselves bound by the law and by our professional code of ethics. Yet the law in some instances mandates practices and procedures that lead us into ethical quagmires. This state of affairs presents us with dilemmas which are not easily resolved by psychologists practicing in schools. The kinds of issues raised by our attempts to practice according to our code of ethics, within the law, seem often to be cumulative, with one feeding on another, until it becomes almost impossible to resolve any single issue without creating still another one. We have deliberately chosen to allow our discussion free rein to present the flavor of our dilemma. We hope to convey not only the content of the issues but also the ways problems of law and practice actually do occur.

An excellent example is apparent from Kuriloff's (Note 1) survey, pointing out differences between practice in urban and rural school districts. According to most state laws, children with handicaps must be classified in large part on the basis of a psychologist's evaluation. City school districts, with their large numbers of children with educational handicaps and their relatively poor psychologist-to-pupil ratio, demand that the psychologist spend the bulk of his time testing for the purpose of classifying children for special education. The psychologist who is interested in moving toward Kuriloff's conception of a broad role definition expresses his dilemma by protesting about his limited assignment. He wishes to convince his superiors that he should not be locked in his office administering WISC-R's to children, that he has other skills that he should be using in intervention and planning for the prevention of educational and emotional problems, and that keeping him from using these skills may be a violation not only of his professional prerogatives but, perhaps, of his ethical responsibilities. These psychologists are likely to have their administrative superiors respond by pointing out what the law says psychologists in the schools *must* do. Many of us get the message that if it were not for the law (and the reimbursement to school districts for psychological services that is often part of the law), school psychologists would not have jobs. Paradoxical it is, to administrators and others, that as school psychologists we are annoyed with the very laws that ensure us employment in the schools. Take away those laws, it is said, and some substantial proportion of school districts would not be willing, voluntarily, to employ us at direct expense to a local board of education. Some school personnel regard us as peripheral or as offering a limited adjunctive school service, a regard that has its basis in another of our interrelated dilemmas. By allowing our efforts to be limited to testing and report writing, calculated to justify a pupil's classification in a particular category of handicap, we tend to perpetuate the view that our value is limited precisely to these functions. Further, our reports and hours of labor are considered relatively useless except for the single sentence in the report that reads "On the basis of Johnny's IQ of X and (we throw in a few other behavior comments which are largely ignored), he is classifiable as Y."

The more we allow ourselves to be used only to satisfy our part in meeting the law requiring classification of children for special education, the more we can be accused of not using our professional skills wisely (ethically?). The more we try to offer expanded services, the more we can be accused of not meeting our legal responsibilities which formed the basis for our initial employment and major service to the school district.

We have a long and continuous history of difficulty based on legislation attempting to correct inequities concerned with educational and other human rights and responsibilities. These troubles have not been related to the morality or justice of the legislation but to the professional implications involved in its implementation. For example, in the 1950's and 1960's a plethora of laws was passed in the several states mandating various psychological services in special education. These laws were designed to direct attention to the truly neglected 10 to 15 % of the school population who needed something special in education. Yet these laws created a demand for psychological services that could not be filled. There were not enough of any kind of psychologists around, let alone well-trained school psychologists. Certification standards, if they existed at all, consisted of minimal requirements. Adoption of minimal requirements in order to get psychologists into the schools so that the law could be implemented led to the quick production of a number of psychometrists whose label of "school psychologist" meant they could administer Binet and Wechsler tests, but were qualified to do little else in the way of psychological functioning. To be a school psychologist meant one could be counted upon to come up with an IQ number. As indicated earlier, neither schools nor most school psychologists were happy with this situation. The schools discovered that giving a child a test did not really change anything. The many children whose IQ labels did not justify special placement remained in the classroom, troubling teachers. Ergo, school psychologists were not worth the salary paid them.

School psychologists, beginning to receive training in psychological functions beyond psychometrics, began offering counseling to individuals or small groups of children, consulting with teachers, and meeting with parents. This branching out of activities led to another dilemma: on the one hand, schools were eager for something that would change nonconforming children; on the other, they were apprehensive about parental-community reaction. To compound matters, the medical profession, here and there, raised serious questions about the ethics of nonphysicians offering "therapy," based on *its* view of ethical and legal constraints of medical practice.

More recently still, that most basic of psychological functions in the schools–testing–has in some instances been specifically outlawed (Steinbock, Beerman, Bellamy, DiRocco, Foss, & Friedland, 1975). Psychologists in the schools have long been concerned about the ethics of using any group tests or the unqualified results of individually administered intelligence tests as the sole determinants to classify children as mentally retarded, but they did not want to forfeit a valuable tool because of its abuses by practitioners not adequately prepared to use it. The resolution of the dramatic confrontation–the desire to redress a wrong through law and the failure to create adequate means to do so–in this instance appears to lead inevitably toward depriving school psychologists of the use of their professional judgment in the matter of judicious use of tests for the best educational placement for children.

If there is a single pervasive characteristic of legislation affecting the practice of psychology, it is that once passed, little is done to ensure the execution of a law in the spirit in which the law was intended.

For instance, most legislation providing psychological services for the purposes of identifying and classifying children who have educational handicaps was instituted by dedicated parent groups beating upon the doors of altruistic or constituency-oriented legislators. The laws were passed. All well and good. The laws told schools there would be financial provision for the necessary psychological and other services to help implement the law. Again, all well and good. But the special education laws in most states were passed with little consideration given to the existing psychologists' competencies to perform the mandated job, for the most part with no consultation with professional psychologists in defining the job, with virtually no consideration of existing training facilities to produce the professionals to do the job, and no provisions for training new personnel needed to execute the laws.

School administrators appealed to state departments of education to help provide the necessary personnel; state departments of education issued all kinds of "provisional," "temporary," and other euphemisms for "inadequately trained" certificates enabling persons to practice in the schools as school psychologists.

The vicious circle is insidious. The law encourages inadequate practice. Inadequate practice leads to criticism of the inadequacy of *all* practitioners, leading to new laws forbidding the practitioner to practice in certain ways necessary to carrying out the law. The question of legislative accountability and the ethics involved in the passage of laws without adequate safeguards for ensuring its effectiveness is a serious national and state problem which goes far beyond our area of immediate interest.

The most recent federal laws dealing with special education reflect the typical circular pattern (Public Law 93–380, Title VI, Part B). First we must identify children for the sake of putting them in special classes. Then, to correct inequities in carrying out the laws, we are told that we should not put children in special classes but should "mainstream" them. Assuredly mainstreaming is an excellent concept, but legislating mainstreaming to counteract the tendency to dump children into special education classes is fraught with problems too, and we submit a dire prediction that the backlash will soon be upon us.

Again, our ability to exercise our professional and ethical judgment is being undermined by legislation. Now that many of us have become involved in mainstreaming, we have found, expectedly, that it works well with some children and at some grade levels, but that there is a need for professional judgment about who, when, and for how long. For example, some children can be mainstreamed successfully in the primary grades, but in the higher grades they are subjected to a variety of complicating conditions which suggest that other educational arrangements may be more desirable.

Other kinds of legislation cause still other dilemmas. A recent law in Pennsylvania (Steinbock, et al., 1975) requires that all children needing special services be identified, but they may not be labeled. How is it possible to *identify* children needing help without sorting out some children as different from others? What means for the identification of children needing help are to be employed, if not some kind of measure of deficit?

As soon as we talk about a measure of deficit, or of identification, we are talking about some kind of "test." Cronbach (1975) reminds us of something many have forgotten—that in the United States the testing movement received great impetus because it was a way of identifying the talented poor. How do we identify those children who have "hidden potential"? With Spanish-speaking children, for example, do we rely on observations (helpful, but unreliable and unstandardized)? Do we use the performance scale of the WISC-R (on which, unfortunately, some Spanish-speaking as well as English-speaking children will perform poorly), or should we use the older Spanish version of the WISC, about which there are serious questions of standardization and appropriateness? We come to the absurd conclusion that the only appropriate measure to use is one on which *no* child performs poorly, or, in other words, does not discriminate. It is illegal to discriminate among children but it is illegal not to identify children who have an educational handicap. What a paradox!

Another problem arises from the special education laws that require a particular label be pinned on a pupil in order for that pupil to receive special educational attention. The unreliability of diagnostic categories has been well demonstrated in psychiatry as well as in psychology, and psychologists find themselves tampering with the rules and regulations governing the laws in their concern for the individual needs of children. Joe may well be classifiable as neurologically impaired, but it would be psychologically unsound for Joe, for the teacher, and for the other children in a particular NI class for him to be placed there. However, the class for the emotionally disturbed, with another teacher and fewer children, has an educational climate in which Joe could fit, both on the basis of his behavior as well as his academic level. Well, is not Joe in some respects also "emotionally disturbed," although he may not meet the exact specifications of the rules governing the special education laws of that state? Joe is assigned to the class for the emotionally disturbed. Is this kind of assignment illegal? Perhaps it is. Is it unethical? We do not think it inevitably is. Inability to act on professional judgment in the interest of improved educational provisions for children is one unfortunate by-product of laws which, in effect, mandate provisions which apply across the board to a category of children.

ORGANIZATIONAL APPROACH TO THE LAW

We have attempted to point out some of the dilemmas and paradoxes created by the proliferation of laws that attempt to mandate ethical professional functioning. Our next task is to try to find some approaches to solutions of the problems, especially as these problems can be approached through professional organizations.

Rationale. The purpose of any professional organization is to identify its members as those who possess a unique and difficult-to-attain set of skills and knowledges and to band together those members for the purpose of protecting and enhancing their interests (Moore, 1970). In the case of psychology, as with other professional organizations concerned with service to the public, the professional organization also assumes the responsibility for protecting the public from incompetent or unethical practice, and to quote directly from the Bylaws of APA (Note 2), "to advance psychology as a science and as a means of promoting human welfare . . . ; by the improvement of the qualifications of psychologists through high standards of professional ethics, conduct, education, and achievement" (p. xi).

To call oneself a professional means that one is committed to a set of normative and behavioral expectations, that the professional is indeed competent to *practice* within the definition of the profession, and that the professional is competent to exercise autonomous judgment and authority in his practice. The professional organization sets the standards for the behavioral expectations, defines the competence, and provides a code of ethics to guide the exercised autonomous judgment and authority in professional practice.

The American Psychological Association is, of course, the professional organization of all psychologists. It consists of such a diversity of particular areas of interests within its membership that there are now 36 divisions, each division representing an interest group. Many divisions have no interest in the practice of psychology as the word "practice" is usually interpreted; these divisions are devoted to psychology as a scientific endeavor. Other divisions are primarily professional in the sense that they apply their knowledge and skills directly to problems presented to them for resolution. Division 16, the Division of School Psychology, is one of the professional divisions of APA. Diversity among the membership explains the various pressures within APA to support or not support certain courses of action in one direction or the other. This state of affairs leads to the kinds of problems associated with any democratic body–slowness of action, interminable deliberation, and compromises based on political manuevering. On the other side of the coin, just as in any democratic organization, the perceived slowness to act is also a brake upon impulsive action, interminable deliberation ensures carefulness of thought, and compromise results in the support of the total body to a commitment made. It is this support from the total body that gives APA its clout when it does decide to act.

For example, for many years APA refused to taint its professional image (and its tax structure) by getting involved in the process of influencing legislation. However, legislation in recent years increasingly has moved in the direction of affecting human welfare, and, as such, has become intimately involved with how psychology is practiced. When legislation began to influence the behavior of psychologists, whether involved in practice or in research activity, the result was a rather dramatic coming together of the various interest groups, resulting in the formation of the Association for the Advancement of Psychology (AAP), separate from APA but supported by it.

AAP's raison d'etre is to watchdog legislation pertinent to psychology, to ensure the input of psychology into proposed legislation, and to try to educate the public and the legislators of the nature of, and need for, a wide variety of psychological services. AAP has, in the short time span of its existence, kept track of the 1,438 bills introduced in the Senate and 6,177 bills introduced in the House of Representatives, of which many had some relevance for professional psychology (AAP Reports Progress, 1975). Its able executive director, Clarence Martin, and small, hard-working staff, depend upon the professional body of psychology to provide the technicalities. For example, one proposed version of the many dealings with National Health Insurance defined the provider of psychological services as a "clinical psychologist." It was impossible to change that word "clinical," but the definition of "clinical" was changed to one broad enough to include any practitioner (including a school psychologist). AAP, with its close surveillance of what goes on in Washington, alerted us about the signing into law of Public Law 930:380 containing the famous Buckley Amendments, and arranged for representatives of Division 16 to be present at Washington hearings to help determine how the Rules and Regulations (interpretation and implementation of the Law) would read. School psychologists were rightly concerned about the effects of the Law's "Rights of parents to have access" upon the confidentiality of their records, another example, incidentally, of how legislation determines ethical practice. The most important point for this discussion, however, is that although it was the representatives of Division 16 who were present at these important meetings, the points those representatives made were perceived as coming from APA, not just a small subsection of school psychologists. Working through a national organization such as APA means that once you can get that diverse body to agree upon certain legislative thrusts, you have the backing of a constituency of 40,000 members. It is worth the effort to get that kind of support.

APA's Bylaws' pledge to improve the qualifications of psychologists through high standards has become a controversial issue as part of the efforts to ensure that the users of psychological services are entitled to the same kind of reimbursement, from private and public insurance organizations, as is available to other health services. The Board of Professional Affairs (BPA) of APA appointed a Committee on Standards to develop a document detailing standards for psychological practice. The various potential reimbursers (insurance agencies) for psychological services have pointed out the existing confusion arising from the fact that there are psychologists and psychologists, only some of whom hold doctorates. The reimbursers point out that there is no such thing as a nondoctoral physician or dentist, and many also point out that their guidelines for reimbursement for mental health services insist that the physician, for example, be a "Boarded psychiatrist" as a way of defining the psychiatrist as eligible to practice a specialty. Reasonably, then, should not psychologists, considering they vary in orientation and specialty, also be "Boarded" (translate, for psychology, to Diplomate status)? The potential reimbursers have in the past been adamant about this point, and it is apparent that this issue is a good example of the need to compromise. If, at this point, APA were to insist that all nondoctoral psychologists are eligible for reimbursement, the whole movement for reimbursement for psychological services will be indefinitely stalemated. Hence the formation of the National Registry (through the American Board of Professional Psychology, ABPP), and the issuance of a set of *Standards* that spell out the doctoral level as that of entry to private, unsupervised practice.

Large numbers of nondoctoral psychologists, especially school psychologists, are understandably disappointed, bitter, and critical of APA. School psychologists' interest group in APA, Division 16, reflected the concern of its constituents in Council, resulting in Council's approval of the *Standards as* representative of APA's pledge to promote standards, but recognition that the *Standards* as currently written do not reflect the actuality of practice in the schools. In January, 1975, BPA was charged to appoint a new Committee on Standards, directing that the new Committee include members from those interest groups within APA who could help amend the *Standards*. Two school psychologists were appointed to that seven-member Committee.

Concern about APA's emphasis on doctoral training for full membership in Association and the belief that school psychology could profit from its own professional interest group led, in 1969, to the formation of the National Association of School Psychologists (NASP). It was the intention of this Association to focus attention on the specific needs of school psychologists by influencing national and state legislation and by working toward the enhancement of the professional interests of school psychologists. In other words, NASP developed a mission for school psychology which in most respects parallels the mission APA has for all psychology.

During its brief history, NASP appears to have been successful in bringing into a national group school psychologists who had not previously been associated with APA, has helped to clarify minimal standards for functioning in schools, and has promoted considerable interest in the specialty. It appears to have been less successful in its efforts to influence federal legislation, perhaps because of the already cited reason that it cannot adequately represent all of psychology, thereby losing some of the strength to be gained by united effort of all of American psychology.

Another function of national organizations to meet their pledge to improve the qualifications of psychologists is through accreditation of training programs. Accreditation is a complicated business which begins with a National Council on Accreditation (NCA), which has specialty accrediting agencies within its overall framework. It is assumed that each professional group is best able to set standards for the training of its professionals. Physicians are responsible for judging the training of physicians, through AMA, dentists through ADA, lawyers through ABA, educators through NCATE (National Council of Accreditation of Teacher Education), psychologists through APA. The fact that school psychologists are psychologists who operate within the educational framework has caused some serious problems of jurisdiction. School psychologists are *certified* to work in the schools by educational agencies, as are teachers and administrators. Many school psychology training programs are housed in colleges of education, and as such are subject to being evaluated by *educators* who are representing NCATE. On the other hand, through APA, school psychology now may be accredited by *psychologists*. APA accredits only doctoral level programs, however, and as a recent survey indicates (Bardon & Wenger, Note 3), the largest number of training programs in school psychology are nondoctoral, and in recent years they are being established primarily in units of universities other than departments of psychology. This thrust has led the National Association of School Psychologists (NASP) to consider alternative means of accrediting nondoctoral school psychology programs. NCATE evaluation does not require doctoral level training, as, of course, most educators are not required to reach that level. The situation at this point is unresolved and may remain so until school psychologists decide wholeheartedly to put themselves in one camp or the other. Are we primarily psychologists? Or are we educators with psychological training, therefore "pupil personnel workers"? The editorial view of the authors is understandably that we are (or should be) psychologists, whose specialty is the application of psychology to school functioning.

Another area of law and professional practice in psychology in which national organizational efforts have been effective has been in response to the plethora of recent laws restricting research on human subjects. The thrust of right to privacy and concern for individual rights is apparent (and probably needed) in legislative efforts to restrict experimentation that might represent invasion of privacy or efforts to coerce or mislead its subjects. The good intentions of some of the proposed legislation, however, results in overrestriction, thereby interfering with legitimate and needed research. Our responsibility to conduct research in an ethical manner and to promote knowledge may, again, be legislated to the detriment of our professional efforts. Overly strict regulation of research practices may be tied to psychology's reluctance to set its own standards in anticipation of potential difficulties. A recent example is the restriction on use of behavior modification in penal institutions (Trotter & Warren, 1974) resulting from reported abuses by a few.

The original version of the "Buckley Amendments" contained stringent restrictions upon research in the schools, in essence making it impossible to conduct longitudinal research by ruling out the collection of "personally identifiable" data. AAP's input into the hearings assured that the interpretation of the law continues to respect the privacy of pupils, but permits the kind of "anonymous" data collection via coding that makes possible correlational and longitudinal research (Public Law 93:380, Note 4).

ORGANIZATIONS AT THE STATE LEVEL

As psychology matures as a profession, it takes its place along with the other, older professions in its efforts to ensure high standards of practice. Licensing by state law is established primarily to protect the public from inadequate practitioners; licensing also protects the image and credibility of the profession. Licensing for psychologists to practice privately is relatively recent, and there are still a few states struggling to get licensing laws passed for psychological practice. The national organization, APA, also helps coordinate the activities at the state level through BPA's Committee on State Legislation (COSL), which provides advice, guidelines, information, and the clout of APA to states on matters of licensing. There is need for national guidelines to ensure uniformity of standards for licensing, but of course states are notoriously autonomous and do not always adopt nationally recommended guidelines. State licensing, however, is the way of the future for eligibility for psychological services to be reimbursed by private or public insurance, and as such should be monitored accordingly. One precautionary suggestion is adoption of the doctoral level as the entry level, but providing for liberal grandfathering of well-qualified, nondoctoral psychologists.

Just as at the national level there is virtue in coordinating activities to ensure the greatest impact upon legislators, at the state level there is need for school psychologists to join with their nonschool professional colleagues and engage in negotiation, compromise, and quid-pro-quo mutual support. Many state school psychological associations, because of perceived conflict of interest, do not formally affiliate with their state psychological association, especially as state psychological associations are affiliates of APA. We wish to point out that despite some current dissenting points of view, in the long run, "If we don't hang together we shall surely hang separately," as one of our founding fathers pointed out.

WHERE DO WE GO FROM HERE?

In summary, it is evident that legislation is increasingly dictating our professional functioning, and in many instances is determining ethical behavior on the part of psychologists. The function of professional organizations, whether at the national or state levels, is to be able to predict *when* and *why* this kind of legislation is being promulgated. The tendency in the past has been for smaller subgroups of organizations to react primarily on a self-serving basis (how does this law affect me?) rather than on taking the long view, resulting in the grim realization that as psychologists we have not been sufficiently stringent in our own self-monitoring. We must stop deluding ourselves by trying to ensure that all the subgroups within psychology are fat and happy; instead we must work toward the kinds of professional practice that are best for the public. In the long run, such practice will be best for the profession.

It is easy to write that working together toward altruistic goals is the solution to the problems of professional practice created by the ever-increasing impact of legislative activity. It is, in fact, a slow, agonizing, evolutionary process whereby competing, yet overlapping factions of a profession eventually find ways to come together toward the solution of mutual goals. In school psychology at the national level, it is necessary for Division 16, as part of APA, and NASP to find improved ways of working together, or it is predictable that we will weaken our ability to influence legislative action which affects our functioning. At the state level the state psychological associations and, where they exist, the state school psychological associations must find ways to work out their differences toward common action when it matters. In both instances the sensitive areas that must be addressed are the entry level for independent professional functioning in psychology, the determination of whether school psychology is primarily a specialty of psychology or education, and the ability of nondoctoral psychologists to have full membership privileges in their national association. These problems cannot even be addressed without the *intent* of all concerned to do so. It is hoped that psychologists may know enough about problem resolution to find ways to work together. It is also hoped that they may care enough about how all professional practice in psychology is affected by national and state law to try to resolve these issues, compromising where possible and seeking ways to cooperate, even while holding to separate principles, on those issues affecting all of us who are psychologists.

REFERENCE NOTES

1. Kuriloff, P. Law, educational reform, and the school psychologist. *Journal of School Psychology* (in press).
2. American Psychological Association. Bylaws of the American Psychological Association. Biographical Directory, Washington, D. C. 1973.
3. Bardon, J. I., & Wenger, R. D. Training in school psychology: Trends during the early 1970's (manuscript submitted for publication, 1975).
4. An act to extend and amend the Elementary and Secondary Education Act, and for other purposes. Public Law 93:380, 93rd Congress, H. R. 69, August 21, 1974.

REFERENCES

AAP reports progress. *AAP Advance,* 1975, *2,* 2.

Cronbach, L. J. Five decades of public controversy over mental testing. *American Psychologist*, 1975, *30*, 1–14.

Moore, W. E. *The professions: Roles and rules*. New York: Russell Sage Foundation, 1970.

Steinbock, E. A., Beermann, L. L., Bellamy, G. T., DiRocco, P., Foss, G., & Friedland, M. Civil rights of the mentally retarded: An overview. *Law and Psychology Review*, 1975, *Spring,* 151–177.

Trotter, S., & Warren, J. Behavior modification under fire. *APA Monitor,* 1974, *5,* 1, 4.

Virginia C. Bennett
Professor of Psychology and Education
Graduate School of Applied and Professional Psychology
Psychology Building, Busch Campus
Rutgers University
New Brunswick, New Jersey 08903

Jack I. Bardon
Professor of Psychology and Education
Graduate School of Applied and Professional Psychology
Psychology Building, Busch Campus
Rutgers University
New Brunswick, New Jersey 08903

Journal of School Psychology
1975 • Vol. 13, No. 4

PROFESSIONAL ETHICS AND LEGAL RESPONSIBILITIES: ON THE HORNS OF A DILEMMA

DONALD N. BERSOFF

Yale Law School

Summary: Through a series of fact situations the author demonstrates that reliance by practicing school psychologists on codes of ethics may lead to legal liability. Five areas are chosen for particular attention: 1) Parents' right to access to records; 2) Informed consent and the right to privacy in research and assessment; 3) Confidentialty of client-clinician communication; 4) Parental refusal of proferred educational services; 5) Treatment of minors without parental consent. Current statutory and case law is reviewed to give practitioners some sense of how the legislature and judiciary view professionals' responsibility in these areas. The article concludes with a discussion of why codes of ethics fail to provide adequate support for psychologists in meeting problems encountered in their everyday functioning and suggests some remedial measures for improving the current codes governing school psychology.

I would like to use as a vehicle for this article a day in the professional life of a school psychologist whom I have named, if readers will forgive, Ethy Kal. She is well-trained, certificated, experienced, intensely motivated to do what is "right," and possesses genuine humanitarian concern for all those with whom she has a personal and professional relationship. She is a member of both the National Association of School Psychologists (NASP) and Division 16 (School Psychology) of the American Psychological Association (APA).

A SCHOOL PSYCHOLOGIST'S HYPOTHETICAL DAY

Dr. Kal's first appointment is with the parents of a child whom the school wishes to place in a class for educably retarded children. Prior to this meeting the parents were asked, and gave, written permission for an evaluation to begin. They were fully informed as to the nature of the intended assessment and the instruments to be administered their son. Now that the assessment is complete, a conference is being held in which Dr. Kal (who evaluated the boy), the child's regular teacher, the prospective special education teacher, the principal, and the parents attend. The child was also invited but declined. After a thorough discussion in which all alternatives are presented, the professional team suggests that a three-month trial in a self-contained classroom would be the most helpful initial placement. The parents are receptive but not convinced that the placement is best for their child. They question the original assessment and ask to look at the Stanford-Binet protocol administered their child. Dr. Kal is not sure that such inspection is appro-

The author wishes to thank Malinda A. Hennen, Ph.D., school psychologist, for her constructive suggestions in the formulation and writing of this article.

priate. A quick scan of the NASP Code of Ethics reveals nothing definitive. She does find Principle II(c) declaring that "the emphasis is on the interpretation and organization rather than the simple passing along of test scores . . . " (NASP, Note 1). Under one of the principles regarding the professional's relationship with parents (Principle V(c)) she finds that school psychologists are urged to secure parental involvement by "frank and prompt reporting . . . of findings obtained in the evaluation of the student" (NASP, Note 1). Searching for more help she checks Principle 13 (Test Security) of the APA Code where s(he) is told that access to psychological tests and other assessment devices are "limited to persons with professional interests who will safeguard their use" (APA, 1963).

On these bases Dr. Kal offers to discuss the test results and their meaning but refuses to show the parents the Binet protocol itself, apologizing for the refusal but claiming the necessity of abiding by his/her profession's codes. The parents insist on seeing the protocol but Dr. Kal, while freely offering to answer all the parents' questions, denies access to the test itself saying that it is only open to inspection by their child's teacher and administrative personnel with a legitimate interest in their son's education. The parents grumble, listen to Dr. Kal's interpretative summary and say they will consider the recommendation of the staff.

At ten o'clock Dr. Kal has a meeting with the Superintendent of Schools. The conference concerns a possible research and intervention program which the district is considering joining. A survey done by a consulting firm has determined that in the school area a significant number of children between the ages of 12 and 18 are involved with drugs who have many personality traits in common. The program involves the administration of questionnaires to junior high school students and their teachers. The students would assess their own personality and identify other students who engage in unusual or inappropriate behavior. They would also be asked questions about their relationship with their mothers and fathers as the survey revealed that certain kinds of parent-child interaction discriminated significantly between drug and nondrug users. Teachers would nominate children who most and least fit certain descriptions, e.g., "This pupil's behavior is unpredictable." The questionnaires would then be returned to a research staff for analysis and from this a list of children having a high probability of becoming drug abusers would be compiled. The final phase of the program would provide intervention through individual and group sessions run by guidance counselors, school psychologists, and other personnel. The program would thus be, as its developers see it, a preventive measure by which the school district could identify potential drug abusers, prepare necessary interventions, and preclude future difficulty.

Dr. Kal has many scientific and ethical concerns about this study. Principle III(b) of the NASP Code implores the school psychologist to respect "the student's right of choice to enter, and participate in services voluntarily," and demands that the psychologist explain the procedures for collecting information and the uses to which the information obtained will be put. Parental contact prior to evaluation is also strongly suggested (Principle V[a]) (NASP, Note 1). APA's Code is just as specific. Principle 7(d) requires that personal information from a client should be obtained "only after making certain that the responsible person is fully aware of the purposes of the . . . evaluation and of the ways in which the information may be used" (APA, 1963).

Dr. Kal inquires as to the psychometric soundness of the instruments. The reliability coefficient (test-retest) is in the .90s. Predictive validity is .85, excellent for a questionnaire. The instrument seems able to identify clearly a majority of teenagers who would eventually use drugs. Dr. Kal is still concerned about the project but thinks that the positive social consequences outweigh the potential harm. S(he) is bolstered in this conclusion by Principle 1(a) of the APA Code: "As a scientist, the psychologist believes that society will be best served when he investigates where his judgment indicates investigation is needed" (APA, 1963). But s(he) continues to feel that informed consent and prior permission is necessary before such a sensitive study and treatment program is begun. S(he) argues for such safeguards at a meeting with the Superintendant. The Superintendant, however, concludes that the administration of the questionnaire is primarily an educational function, like the giving of standardized achievement tests, and thus does not require prior permission. Dr. Kal patiently explains the difference, convincing the Superintendant to draft a letter to all parents. He, in turn, delegates the task to him/her and the following is the result of that effort:

> Dear Parent:
>
> This letter is to inform you that this fall we are initiating a Drug Program the aim of which is to identify children who may be susceptible to drug abuse and to intervene with concrete measures to help these children. Diagnostic testing will be a part of this program and will provide data enabling the prevention program to be specific and positive.
>
> This program will be started in Grade 8. We ask your support and cooperation in this program and assure you of the confidentiality of these studies. If you wish to examine or receive further information regarding the program, please feel free to contact the principal in your school. If you do not wish your child to participate in the program, please notify your principal of this decision.

Dr. Kal went to lunch feeling virtuous and highly ethical. S(he) had confronted the administration and forced it to protect the rights of students and parents.

The initial appointment in the afternoon is with a high school student Dr. Kal has been seeing in psychotherapy for some time. Dr. Kal feels s(he) could be more effective as a school psychologist by consulting with teachers and administrators rather than concentrating on one-to-one relationships but s(he) also knows that in a few well-selected instances providing counseling is helpful to the client while it hones his/her own clinical skills. S(he) had been trained in a more traditional psychodynamic approach and while s(he) has, in the past few years, expanded his/her skills to include behavioral and organizational development techniques, s(he) is competent to provide, where s(he) thinks it appropriate, a more exploratory kind of intervention.

The student s(he) is seeing, an 18 year old senior, had come to him/her voluntarily and therapy was proceeding well. Today, however, the student tells his therapist that he is going to kill a girl, unnamed but readily identifiable by Dr. Kal, when the girl returns from a mid-semester vacation with her parents in a few weeks. Dr. Kal is at a loss; s(he) does not want to destroy the confidential relationship with the client but judges that his threat is genuine. S(he) makes another appointment with the young man for the next morning and, as before, consults the code of ethics. APA's Principle 6(a) proves helpful. It says, "Information received in confidence is revealed only after most careful deliberation and when there is clear and imminent danger to an individual or to society, and then only to appropriate professional workers or public authorities" (APA, 1963). So, Dr. Kal confers with an experienced psychologist s(he) sees for therapy supervision. The supervisor agrees that the authorities should be told as there certainly appears to be a "clear and imminent danger" to the young woman. Dr. Kal calls the police and requests that the student be taken into custody for possible commitment. She learns soon after that the police have found the student but, satisfied that he is rational, have released him on his promise to stay away from the girl. Dr. Kal wonders if s(he) should call the threatened young woman but is persuaded not to by the strong language of Principle 6 that such actions would be inappropriate.

On the heels of this incident follows a special education placement meeting. Dr. Kal had evaluated a third grade girl and found her to be a prime candidate for the "Behavior Disorders" class. The girl has been constantly bothering other children, is verbally abusive to the teacher, and, despite measured intelligence in the "Superior" range, is not yet able to read even first grade material. Her potential teacher is excellent. Almost all of this teacher's students have increased in both academic and social skills. Rarely does a child stay in her class for longer than the academic year before being successfully reintegrated into the regular class. The teacher-pupil ratio is 8-1 and there is little doubt that the young girl would benefit by placement. The parents gave permission for an evaluation but have adamantly refused placement. The first letter from the school was returned by the parents with a message scribbled saying, "We don't want our child in a class with crazy kids." Five attempts have been made to arrange a parent conference to no avail. The school social worker has made a special trip to the home, in the evening, but once identified, was refused entrance. The school sent a registered letter to the parents stating that their daughter would be placed in a special class if the parents did not send a return letter refusing permission for such placement.

Today's meeting is being held 10 days after that letter was sent. No reply has been received. The Placement Team asks Dr. Kal what to do next. Principle II(d) of NASP's ethical code is helpful but not decisive, offering, "Where a situation occurs in which there are divided or conflicting interests . . . the school psychologist is responsible for working out a pattern of action which assures mutual benefit and protection of rights for all concerned" (NASP, Note 1). Dr. Kal reviews the faithful efforts to secure permission for placement from the parents, the disruption the girl is causing, the harm to the girl herself as she falls further and further behind despite her good genetic endowment, and the proven benefits that placement offers. On these bases, s(he) recommends placement in the best interests of the student and the school.

There is one final chore on this long day. A 14 year old female at the junior high school has asked to see Dr. Kal. S(he) drives over to the small office provided him/her at the school and arrives in time to meet a very sad-looking young person. "I need to talk to you but I won't unless you promise not to tell my parents," is the student's initial outburst. Dr. Kal replies that s(he) could not make that promise, that there are limits to confidentiality, and that there might be things that s(he) would be bound to reveal, such as a serious intent to commit suicide or to harm someone else. The student tells Dr. Kal that it is nothing like that; she only wants to talk and get some information. Having communicated the restrictions of confidentiality as required by APA Principles 7(d) and 8[1] as well as NASP's Principle III(b)(c),[2] Dr. Kal feels s(he) can now hear what the troubled pupil has to say. The problem is not unfamiliar. The adolescent became pregnant two months ago and has been afraid to tell her parents. She and her boy friend have saved enough money for an abortion but do not know where to have it performed and she asks Dr. Kal to recommend a safe place. The school psychologist is now faced with another quandry: Should s(he) inform the girl's parents? APA's code is not very helpful. True, Principle 8 discusses the need to inform the person's custodian when the client is not competent to evaluate the circumstances which might influence entrance into the relationship to begin with. But, this young woman seems to understand the limits of confidentiality, certainly seems competent, and has, in fact, made specific plans to alleviate her difficulty. NASP's code urges that the school psychologist take into account the rights of parents, as well as "the expanding self-independence and mature status of the student," (Principle III(d), NASP, Note 1) but that reminder is only in regard to informing the student of the rationale for sharing information. Nevertheless, it certainly seems as if becoming pregnant, saving money, and planning for an abortion indicates independence as well as growing maturity. Thus, despite gnawing doubts that s(he) should inform the parents, Dr. Kal concludes that the right of a maturing teenager to make decisions concerning those things in which she has a direct and personal interest transcends the right and need of the parents to know (who might punish the girl and refuse to allow the abortion). Thus, s(he) gives the student the name and addresses of three reputable abortion clinics. But, when the girl asks if she is doing the right thing in terminating the pregnancy,

[1]Principle 7(d): The psychologist who asks that an individual reveal personal information in the course of interviewing, testing, or evaluation, or who allows such information to be divulged to him, does so only after making certain that the responsible person is fully aware of the purposes of the interview, testing, or evaluation and of the ways in which the information may be used.

Principle 8: The psychologist informs his prospective client of the important aspects of the potential relationship that might affect the client's decision to enter the relationship.

[2]Principle III(b): The school psychologist explains to the student who the psychologist is, what the psychologist does, and why the student is being seen. The explanation includes the uses to be made of information obtained, procedures for collecting the information, persons who will receive specific information, and any obligation the psychologist has for reporting specified information. This explanation should be in language understood by the student.

Principle III (c): The school psychologist informs the student of the rationale for sharing information. The course of action proposed takes into account the rights of the student, the rights of the parent, the responsibilities of the school personnel, and the expanding self-independence and mature status of the student.

Dr. Kal says that s(he) can not make that decision for her and that if she has doubts, she should consult with her parents.

Our hero(ine) goes home and, reflecting on the day, feels good about the work s(he) has accomplished. Conscientiously consulting the codes of ethics of both professional organizations to which s(he) belongs s(he) has dealt reasonably with the demanding parents who wanted to see the Binet protocol; has averted possible trouble with the community over the drug prevention program; has used good judgment in calling the police even though it might damage the relationship with the therapy client; has served the best interests of the child and school, while giving the parents every possible benefit of the doubt, by placing the third grader in the special class; and has acted with great candor and discretion in counseling the pregnant teenager. And so, Dr. Kal rewards him/herself in what s(he) considers a suitable way and forgets about the day.

Two months later Dr. Kal is called into the Superintendent's office. On the desk are copies of four lawsuits and a letter from HEW. HEW is threatening to withdraw all funds provided to the school system by the Office of Education because of a violation of a federal law requiring that the school allow access by parents to their children's school records. A parent of one of the eighth grade students is requesting an order by the federal district court to stop the drug prevention program as a violation of the first, fourth, fifth, ninth, and fourteenth amendments of the U.S. Constitution. The parents of the girl his/her therapy client had threatened is suing. The student had indeed carried out his threat eight weeks after he had revealed his intent to Dr. Kal. The parents of the dead girl are requesting monetary damages alleging that Dr. Kal, the school, Dr. Kal's supervisor, and the police were negligent in failing to warn the girl of the student's threat. The parents of the third grader are complaining that the school is stigmatizing and branding their daughter by placing her in a class for behavior disordered children without their permission. They are seeking an injunction preventing placement plus money damages. Finally, the parents of the pregnant adolescent are also asking compensation, claiming that Dr. Kal is guilty of the sort of enticement (a civil wrong involving the interruption of the relationship between parent and child) for failure to inform the parents that their daughter was being seen for counseling and for giving addresses of abortion clinics when the parents did not believe that abortion was moral.

Dr. Kal's ethically-oriented behavior may cost the school district close to a million dollars.

THE LAW AND ITS EFFECT ON THE FUNCTIONING OF SCHOOL PSYCHOLOGISTS

Taken as a whole the fact situations described demonstrate an anxiety-provoking phenomenon: reliance on personal morality and codes of ethics may lead to unanticipated and unwished for legal consequences. Some of these consequences may be the result of ignorance of the law and some the failure to predict courts' decisions as judges face conflicts never before litigated. Taken individually, they represent five areas in which the law is currently having profound impact on the functioning of psychologists and other school people. These areas can be identified as: (1) Parents' right to access to records; (2) Informed consent and the right to privacy in research and assessment; (3) Confidentiality of client-clinician communication; (4) Parental refusal of profferred educational services; (5) Treatment of minors without parental consent.

The remainder of this article contains a summary of the statutory and case law within these areas and attempts to explain why carefully considered codes of ethics fail to provide adequate support for psychologists in meeting the problems encountered in their everyday functioning.

Parental Access to Records. For all intents and purposes, parental access to records is now governed by what is popularly known as the "Buckley Amendment,"[3] a section of the federal law extending and amending the Elementary and Secondary Education Act (ESEA) of 1965. The requirements of the new law are designed to protect the privacy of parents and students. It provides that all educational institutions which receive funds under any federal program administered by the U.S. Office of Education must allow parents of students both access to official records directly related to their child and an opportunity for a hearing to challenge those records on the grounds that they are inaccurate, misleading, or otherwise inappropriate. It is the duty of the school to notify parents of these rights. In addition, the law requires that institutions obtain written consent of parents before releasing to third parties personally identifiable data about students from records. These parental rights transfer to public school students when they become 18 years of age and to all students, regardless of age, attending postsecondary educational institutions. The ultimate penalty for failure to comply is termination of funds to school systems which have a policy or practice contrary to the intent of the law.

The Buckley Amendment created immediate confusion because of the ambiguous language sprinkled throughout. One of the most unclear points was what constituted an educational record. The meaning was obscure in the original version. Later revisions published in the Federal Register (January 6, 1975) distinctly *excluded* from the term "records of institutional, supervisory, and administrative personnel and educational personnel ancillary thereto which are in the sole possession of the maker thereof and which are not accessible or revealed to any other person except a substitute" [p. 1210]. This exclusion was anticipated by Trachtman (1972) when he suggested, in a more comprehensible form, that a record be considered as "anything put in writing for others to see" [p. 45].

The arcane statutory language seemed to indicate that anything which the school psychologist did not show to anyone else could be protected from parental inspection. This could certainly include a Binet protocol or any other raw data (i.e., Bender drawings, TAT responses, etc.). However, in a joint statement issued by Sens. Buckley and Pell, which accompanied the amendments in the Federal Register there is some evidence that such material

[3] More formally, the Buckley Amendment is section 438 of the General Education Provisions Act (Title IV of Pub. L. 90–247, as amended), added by section 513, Pub. L. 93–380 (enacted August 21, 1974), and amended by Senate Joint Resolution 40 (Sen. J. Res. 40) (1974).

may not be protected: "[I]f a child has been labeled mentally or otherwise retarded and put aside in a special class or school, parents would be able to review materials in the record which led to this institutional decision . . . to see whether these materials contain inaccurate information or erroneous evaluations about their child" [p. 1213].

It is a legal rule of thumb that language in a statute ordinarily controls its meaning, intent, and application. Thus, one could make the argument that a test protocol in the sole possession of the school psychologist would not be accessible to parents, allowing the practitioner to conform to APA's Code Principle 13 (test stimuli limited to professionals). However, another rule of statutory interpretation holds that when a law's words are ambiguous, the meaning given to them by the drafters is entitled to great weight. As a result, parents could contend that the questions on an individual intelligence test and the child's responses to them led to the school's decision to label and place the child in an EMR class and thus should be inspectable.

It is interesting to note in this regard that the latest draft proposal by an APA committee revising the Code of Ethics has altered principle 13 considerably. Under a proposed Principle 8 (Utilization of Assessment Techniques) test users are urged to "take any precautions they can to protect test security but not at the expense of an individual's right to understand the basis for decisions that adversely affect that individual or that individual's dependents" (APA, Note 2). The proposal thus shifts the emphasis from protection of the profession and its devices to protection of the consumers and clients of the professional, a stance advocated by many writers (Bersoff, 1973; McClelland, 1973; Roston, 1975).

Informed Consent and Privacy in Research and Assessment. The facts concerning the drug prevention program are taken from *Merriken v. Cressman* (Note 3), an actual case recently decided by a federal district court in Pennsylvania. The court considered the program violative of students' right to privacy and viewed it as a usurpation of the exclusive privilege of parents since the program was intended to be administered without the knowing, intelligent, voluntary, and aware consent of the parents. The letter requesting parental permission to engage in the study (quoted verbatim in the text of the hypothetical situation) was deridingly compared to a Book of the Month Club solicitation in which parent's silence would be construed as acquiescence. The letter was also criticized as a selling device in which parents were being convinced to allow children to participate rather than as an objective document that told parents of the potentially negative features and dangerous aspects of the program. Furthermore, the program contained no provision for student consent and no data were to be provided whereby students could make an informed decision about participating.

The letter referred to confidentiality but the court found that the school had no way of insuring that information would not be passed on to third parties. In fact, the program contemplated a massive data bank in which information related to specific students would be disseminated to principals, guidance counselors, athletic coaches, social workers, the PTA, and school board members. There was no absolute assurance that data gathered would not be accessible to authorities with subpoena power.

While the court acknowledged that the data might be obtained with great precision it was concerned about those who would be inaccurately labeled as drug abusers (the false positives). The failure to guarantee confidentiality would compound the problems of mislabeling and treatment by inexperienced personnel. It thus ruled that "when a program talks about labeling someone as a particular type and such label could remain with him for the remainder of his life, the margin of error must be almost nil" [p. 920].

The court was particularly critical of the invasion of privacy represented by the questions which sought to investigate family relationships. It equated the right of privacy to that of free speech and asserted that "the fact that students are juveniles does not in any way invalidate their right to assert their Constitutional right to privacy" [p. 918].[4]

Finally, it weighed all the interests at stake and concluded:

> The Court, in balancing the right of an individual to privacy and the right of the Government to invade that privacy for the sake of the public interest, strikes the balance in favor of the individual . . . . In short, the reasons for this are that the test itself and the surrounding results of that test are not sufficiently presented to both the child and the parents, as well as the Court, as to its authenticity and credibility in fighting the drug problem in this country. There is too much of a chance that the wrong people for the wrong reasons will be singled out and counselled in the wrong manner [p. 921].

Ten years ago Reubhausen and Brim (1965) asserted that "[i] t requires no Cassandra to predict lawsuits by parents, and a spate of restrictive legislation, if those who administer . . . tests in schools—even for the most legitimate of scientific purposes—do not show a sensitive appreciation for both individual and group claims to a private personality" [p. 1194]. Their prediction has come true in both respects; *Merriken* illustrates the lawsuit and section 514 (amending section 439) of P.L. 93–380 (Note 4) illustrates the restrictive legislation. Under this further amendment to ESEA "All instructional material . . . which will be used in connection with any research or experimentation program or project shall be available for inspection by the parents or guardians of the children engaged in such program or project."

The lesson that school personnel must learn is that the private worlds of students can be invaded only where there has been adequate disclosure and informed consent. Both the recently adopted NASP Code and the draft revision of the APA Code more clearly recognize the necessity for fuller involvement by those directly affected by experimental and therapeutic procedures. Principle III of the NASP Code states: "The school psychologist recognizes the obligation to the student, and respects the student's right of

[4] For other cases in which children's rights in schools have been considered see Wood v. Strickland, 95 S. Ct. 992 (1975) (school officials not immune from liability for money damages if they know or reasonably should have known that the action they take within their sphere of official responsibility violates the constitutional rights of the students affected or if they take action with the malicious intention to cause a deprivation of constitutional rights or other injury to students); Goss v. Lopez, 95 S. Ct. 729 (1975) (students entitled to informal hearing before short term suspension); Tinker v. Des Moines Ind. School Dist., 393 U.S. 503 (1969) (students have right to free speech unless it produces substantial and material disruption of school discipline).

choice to enter, and participate in services voluntarily" (NASP, Note 1). In later provisions it outlines the rudiments of informed consent. Principle 6 (Welfare of the Consumer) of APA's draft requires that "psychologists insure that consumers are fully informed as to the purpose and nature of any procedure for evaluation, treatment, or education and they acknowledge the right of clients and students of freedom of participation without coercion" (APA, Note 2). There are practical barriers to genuine informed consent (see generally, Katz, 1972, pp. 609–674) but there is, increasingly, a duty that researchers and clinicians attempt to reach that ideal by more fully disclosing all aspects of their proposed interventions (see Recent Cases, 1974).

Confidentiality of Client Communication.[5] A case decided late in 1974, *Tarasoff v. Regents of University of California* (Note 5), will have profound impact on therapist-client relationships. The facts parallel those outlined in the situation in which Dr. Kal was working with a student bent on murdering a young woman. In the actual case, a client had admitted and subsequently carried out an intent to do the same. The parents of the victim sued the school's governing body, the therapist, and his supervisors, as well as the campus police. For purposes here, only the suit against the therapist need be elaborated on. The parents of the victim claimed that the psychologist had a duty to warn their daughter of the student's threat.

The clinician defended against the action on two grounds. First, he pointed out that while therapy patients often express thoughts of violence they rarely carry out them out; the very nature of psychotherapy actuates clients to voice this kind of ideation. Second, he argued that free and open communication is essential in psychotherapy and that unless clients are assured that information revealed will be held in strict confidence they will be reluctant to make the full disclosure on which successful treatment depends.

The court acknowledged the validity of the psychologist's arguments but found them unpersuasive. It agreed that therapists should not be encouraged routinely to reveal threats of violence to acquaintances of the client. It recognized that the singling out of those few clients whose threats of violence present a serious danger and weighing that against the danger of harm to the client which might result from the revelation involved a decision of exceptional expertise and judgment. But, the court analogized those decisions to all those delicate and demanding judgments that professionals regularly render and concluded that "whatever difficulties the courts may encounter in evaluating the expert judgments of other professions, those difficulties cannot justify total exoneration from liability" [p. 136]. As to the necessity of open communication, the court conceded "the public interest in supporting effective treatment . . . and in protecting the rights of patients to privacy . . . . [p. 136]." However, it concluded, in a statement likely to be oft-quoted, "that the public policy favoring protection of the

[5]This discussion should not be confused with the doctrine of privileged communication which permits clients to prevent certain mental health professionals named by statute from testifying in court about communications revealed within the context of a therapy relationship. For a full discussion of privileged communication and school psychologists see McDermott (1972).

confidential character of patient-psychotherapist communication must yield in instances in which disclosure is essential to avert danger to others. The protective privilege ends where the public peril begins" [p. 137].

The *Tarasoff* decision, while only legally binding on practitioners in California, will affect the future functioning of all psychologists (and their clients), though the exact consequences are not yet clear. One could predict a greater number of involuntary commitments and overdiagnoses in an attempt to protect against potential liability. Psychotherapists may find themselves in conflicts never conceived of by Lewin as they attempt to reconcile their own personal morality and training regarding confidentiality, the vague reminders of their professional codes of ethics which warn of the consequences of violating the moral and legal standards of the community, and the developing legal requirements which demand complex decision-making and balancing between client and public interests. (See also, Simmons, Monahan, Whiteley, & Whiteley, 1975).

One burden, however, becomes clear. Clinicians must disclose to potential clients the limits of confidentiality. They cannot blithely insure secrecy. While psychologists will certainly incur the risk of discouraging therapy relationships, such an encounter cannot be undertaken ethically unless the clinician acknowledges, prior to the beginning of therapy, that certain information cannot be kept in confidence and may be revealed, not only to public authorities but to private third parties who might be the target of the communication. There is no wish to exaggerate the impact of *Tarasoff.* It must be remembered that the decision was rendered in the context of a violent taking of life and it is difficult to predict to what extent the holding of the case will be applied when clients express threats less dangerous than homicide. But, the decision highlights the reality that there are explicit limits to client-clinician privacy and that this relationship is not immune from the scrutiny of society (Fleming & Maximov, 1974).

Parental Refusal of Proffered Educational Services. The conflict represented in the decision to place a third grader in a class for behavior disordered children despite absence of parental permission is not uncommon. It symbolizes the struggle between parents, who have the right to the custody and care of their children, and the school, who has been given the duty to educate children according to its best professional judgment.

In the main, parents have been afforded more protection by the courts than have schools. The family unit has been insulated from state intervention by a long series of Supreme Court decisions. In 1925, for example, the Court called an Oregon statute requiring parents to send their children to public schools, to the exclusion of private alternatives, an "unreasonable interfer[ence] with the liberty of parents and guardians to direct the upbringing and education of children under their control" (*Pierce v. Society of Sisters,* Note 6). More recently, and more pertinently, courts have ruled that parents must first give permission before their children's educational status may be changed (*Pennsylvania Ass'n for Retarded Children v. Commonwealth* (Note 7); *Mills v. Board of Education* (Note 8) and suits in many other states spawned by these two landmark cases). The rights won vary from state to state but generally parents are now required to receive written notice of any proposed changes in status, the reasons for the proposed changes, the opportunity for a hearing at which parents may challenge the school's recommendations and present evidence to substantiate the validity of alternate choices, the right to legal representation to advocate the interests of parents and children, the right to examine records before the hearing, the right to appeal the decision to the state courts, and the right to periodic review of the appropriateness of their child's assignment. Thus, these procedures now prevent unilateral decision-making by the school, insure greater parental involvement, and reaffirm the assumption that parents are at least equally capable as the school staff in deciding what is best for their children (Goldman, 1972).

Parent power, however, is not absolute and there is no question that courts will intervene in family relationships when they consider that children's interests counterbalance those of their parents. For example, in 1901 the Indiana Supreme Court, in upholding its state's compulsory education laws against a challenge by parents that the laws were an unauthorized invasion of their rights said:

> The natural rights of a parent to the custody and control of his . . . child are subordinate to the power of the State . . . . The welfare of the child and the best interests of a society require that the state shall exert its sovereign authority to secure to the child the opportunity to acquire an education . . . . No parent can be said to have the right to deprive his child of the advantages so provided. (State v. Bailey, Note 9)

Similarly, states have required that children receive blood transfusions, vaccinations to enable them to attend school, and other forms of treatment against parental wishes when it was thought such intervention served the child. The clearest present-day examples of the state's power to interfere in family relationships are child abuse reporting statutes, now extant in almost every state, which allow school officials, among others, to report parents they suspect of beating their children.

Given this balance between parents' right to direct the upbringing of their children and the right of the state to intervene when it feels children's best interests are at stake, how might the school proceed when a parent refuses to abide by sound decision-making by competent school personnel? The presumption that parents are the best custodians for their children is not a conclusive one and can be rebutted on convincing evidence that parents are unable, or refuse, to care for the physical or emotional needs of their children. Thus, parents are subject to examination of their fitness and may lose custody when it can be shown that they are guilty of legal neglect[6] ; in some instances they may retain physical custody but lose the right to make certain decisions about their children when the neglect is restricted, e.g., consent to emergency surgery.

In the face of the parents' consistent refusal to give written permission for placement, their failure to attend conveniently-timed placement hearings, and

[6] Generally, neglect refers to the failure to exercise the care that the circumstances justly demand, embracing wilful as well as unintentional disregard. See 42 *Am.Jur. 2d* Infants § 55 (1969).

the school's firm belief that its decisions is the most advantageous for the child involved, it would be the right of the school administrators to initiate neglect proceedings and obtain a judicial determination that their decision is indeed the one most likely to enhance the functioning of the child. In reality, then, school psychologists cannot be solely responsible for working out a pattern of action which will protect everyone's rights. To engage in unilateral decision-making, no matter how benevolently conceived, which will affect significant interests of parents and children is to make school psychologists vulnerable to justifiable litigation.

Treatment of Minors Without Parental Consent. Dr. Kal's interaction with the pregnant teenager surfaces the tension between the right of parents to be informed about and give permission for their children to enter counseling relationships and the right of adolescents to seek professional help when their interests may be adverse to those of their parents.

The statutory and case law is presently in the process of affording adolescents greater freedom to seek medical and psychological help without the necessity of receiving parental permission, a change advocated by many writers and legal scholars in recent years (Foster & Freed, 1972; Holt, 1974; Kleinfeld, 1970, 1971; Wald, 1974). Many states now have statutes permitting minors to give valid consent to treatment for venereal disease, and some, like California, do not require parental consent for abortion. Maryland recently passed a law providing that a minor has the same capacity as an adult to consent to medical treatment if he or she is either eighteen years of age, a high school graduate, married, if he or she seeks treatment or advice concerning venereal disease or contraception, and in the case of females, if she is a mother (see Note, 1975). It has also passed a similar statute permitting those sixteen years of age or over to consent to treatment for emotional disorders but potential clients are restricted to receiving this help from medical personnel (Note, 1971).

Despite these developments, the right of adolescents to seek help by giving valid consent is far from universal and is presently confined to certain modes of intervention by certain classes of practitioners. There may be ample justification in the legal literature in support of the right of young persons to secure treatment without parental permission but until that right is won school systems and school psychologists may continue to be vulnerable to civil suits.

In the specific fact situation presented Dr. Kal acted reasonably. S(he) provided information but did not advocate that the young woman act against her parents' wishes and, in fact, urged that she consult with her parents if she was not sure about the appropriateness of her intended plan. Thus, liability in an enticement action in cases like this would be rare. However, psychologists are more vulnerable when they engage in such positive action as harboring children, finding them a place to stay, or persuading them to leave parental control (Note, 1971).

Dr. Kal's immunity from suit is not so clear if s(he) participates in long-term counseling or psychotherapy without parental approval, especially where the student may be divulging private information about her family. Whether or not Dr. Kal is indeed liable, the point to be made here is that school psychologists, like other school people, must be sensitive to the rights of all concerned and the requirements of the law in the jurisdictions in which they are employed. At the same time that school psychologists may advocate increasing autonomy for children and the latter's right to be directly involved when their personal interests are at stake, psychologists must also be aware of the constraints on practitioners' behavior that the law has imposed.

WHY CODES OF ETHICS FAIL

It should be evident by this time that codes of ethics and the law may present competing demands to the school psychologist. It is not so clear, however, why this phenomenon should exist. One would expect that the law would provide only minimal standards and require less exacting behavior than idealistic codes of ethics designed to guide the conduct of highly trained, carefully selected, service-oriented professionals. Several factors may be responsible for this anomaly.

A basic reason for the failure of ethical codes to provide adequate bases for behavior is their ethnocentrism. Ethics "refer to the way a group of associates define their special responsibility to one another and to the rest of the social order in which they work" (K. Erikson, 1967, p. 367). Thus, codes represent the professional group's point of view and are rarely developed with help from the consumers who receive the professional's services. Psychologists may be living under the false presumption that their ethic is shared by the people they serve. As Nettler (1959) has pointed out, "When the student of behavior works in a . . . community, he cannot assume that his scientifically honorable intentions will be considered morally justifiable by those whom he seeks to help" [p. 683].

Another fundamental problem is that ethical principles are formulated on such an abstract level that they merely provide general guides to actual behavior (Fox, 1959); practitioners rarely understand how these principles are to be applied in specific situations. Enforcement procedures do not provide for the dissemination of decisions arrived at by ethics committees whose judgments and recommendations are made known only to the profession and is limited to those instances when a member has been expelled for a violation. As a consequence, codes may be seen as meaningless rules extraneous to the everyday functioning of the practitioner.

A corollary outcome is that the value of codes may be perceived solely as a means of providing practitioners with a symbol that they are truly professionals, not merely employees, who thereby have a legitimate claim to autonomy. One of the traditional hallmarks of a profession (along with selective recruitment, extended training, and controlled entrance to practice) is a code of ethics which emphasizes devotion to service, concern for the client, and the positive attributes of its adherents (Becker, 1962). With a code in hand and elaborate procedures for its enforcement, the profession may feel that it is now entitled to the trust and confidence of the public it serves. But, as Friedson (1970) has indicated, a code of ethics "has no necessary relationship to the actual behavior of members of the occupation . . . . In this sense, a code of ethics may be seen as one of many methods an occupation may use to induce general belief in the ethicality of its members, without necessarily bearing directly on individual ethicality" [p. 187].

A most painful possibility is that our ethical codes are but hollow symbols of a myth of professionalism. Psychology's self-image as a profession may not be matched by the perception of the real world, a hypothesis even more applicable to school psychology. Most of applied psychology may be little more than a variety of unproven traditional conceptions supplemented by quite variable clinical judgments (Friedson, 1970). Certainly, professional psychology does not yet offer universally-accepted, systematically-developed, scientifically-grounded solutions to practical problems. As long as it appears to courts and to the public that psychology is a cacophony of competing claims to workable procedures, the judgment of its members, regardless of the profession's high-minded ethical standards, will be open to challenge. Psychology is fragmented into many different schools each espousing its own theoretical orientation, a state of affairs which may motivate research and enliven the professional journals but which may inspire little confidence in society. With the field so divided it is not difficult to explain why codes of ethics remain vague and abstract and why a wide variety of specific behavior is tolerated. But, while psychology may permit different interpretations of its ethical guidelines, the courts may not be so benevolent. They do not find it all difficult to disregard a profession's claim to autonomy when the behavior of its practitioners is perceived to interfere with the rights of individuals or the public at large.

School psychologists are particularly vulnerable to increased inspection and control by the courts as they become implicated in litigation in which their competency to assess, classify, and treat youngsters is at issue (e.g., Hobson v. Hansen, Note 10; Stewart v. Philips, Note 11). Nowhere has the school psychologist been more castigated than in *Merriken v. Cressman* (Note 3), the drug program case. The court condemned the program, in part, because it felt that "untrained" personnel (among them school psychologists) were to administer the personality questionnaires and provide the therapeutic intervention. It relied on a rather inflammatory article (Sheerer & Roston, 1971) to support its argument:

> In all probability [the average American parent] is not clear regarding the qualifications of the school "psychologist" who is likely to hold a master's degree in school psychology, not from the psychology department of a college or university, but from an education school or department. Chances are great he has not had significant supervision in a hospital, or outpatient clinic, or from a clinical psychologist or psychiatrist. He is likely to be considered "untrained" by the persons that parents have in mind when they "picture" a psychologist. . . . [p. 115]

School psychologists can no doubt rebut the false assumptions in the quoted excerpt but the painful reality is that school psychologists' claims to competence and professional status have been seriously questioned.

It is apparent that psychology's codes are insufficient protections against increased scrutiny by the courts. The fact that expulsion by its professional organizations is rare may be an indication, not that its members are acting ethically, but that there has been a failure to develop meaningful and contemporary codes. Many of APA's principles are irrelevant to the institutional practitioner like the school psychologist. To satisfy varying and often conflicting constituencies, committees whose responsibility it is to revise codes often take a long time to accomplish the task. The APA has been at work since 1972 redrafting its code and as of this writing (June, 1975) the work has not yet been completed. Leisurely code revision may not reflect adequately the changing demands of the law.

SOME REMEDIAL SUGGESTIONS

A number of fundamental changes may be in order if school spychologists and professional psychologists in general, are to become less vulnerable to litigation and more reliant on workable codes of ethics. To reduce ethnocentrism, it may be helpful for future committees, whose charge it is to rework existing codes, to make parents, children, school officials, and others who will be directly affected by the actions of professionals, integral parts of their membership. To make codes more pertinent and applicable, it may be helpful to consider publishing cases heard by ethics committees. The cases could be collected and printed in much the same way judicial decisions are currently collected. The reports could include the facts involved (with anonymity assured where appropriate), the precise issues in question, the decision of the committee, and the rationale for its judgment. In this way students and practitioners alike would gain heightened awareness of the myriad ethical problems faced by their colleagues and would learn consensually-arrived-at techniques for preventing or remediating such problems.

Psychologists may need to expose themselves more freely to the professional scrutiny and criticism of their colleagues. Acting in a vacuum tends to develop an exaggerated sense of self-correctness. Such conduct makes practitioners assailable when their work is subjected to close examination by courts and attorneys who are not likely to defer to opinion, reputation or professional aura of "expert" on the witness stand (see Ziskin, 1975). This is a time when many professionals are experiencing searching inquiry into their behavior. Courts, particularly, have become less tolerant of claims to autonomy and are less willing to accept self-regulation by professionals as those society have trusted are shown to be untrustworthy. It may now be more appropriate for professional psychologists to begin to collaborate more fully with those with whom they interact and serve. Mutual participation in decision-making in which client and clinician accept each other as equals in the search for solutions (Bersoff, 1973, in press; Fischer, 1970; Szasz & Hollander, 1956) may diminish mistrust, conflict, and litigation.

REFERENCE NOTES

1. National Association of School Psychologists. *Principles for professional ethics,* 1974 (Mimeo).
2. American Psychological Association. *Revision of APA ethical standards* (Draft #7). July, 1975 (Mimeo).
3. *Merriken v. Cressman,* 364 F.Supp. 913 (E.D. Pa. 1973).
4. P.L. 93–380, August, 21, 1974.

5. *Tarasoff v. Regents of University of California,* 13, C.3d 177, 529 P.2d 553, 118 Cal. Rptr. 129 (1974).
6. *Pierce v. Society of Sisters,* 268 U.S. 510 (1925).
7. *Pennsylvania Ass'n for Retarded Children v. Commonwealth,* 334 F.Supp. 1257 (E.D. Pa. 1971); 343 F.Supp. 279 (E.D. Pa. 1972).
8. *Mills v. Board of Education,* 348 F.Supp. 855 (D.D.C. 1972).
9. *State v. Bailey,* 157 Ind. 324, 329–330, 61 N.E. 730, 731–732 (1901).
10. *Hobson v. Hansen,* 269 F.Supp. 401 (D.D.C. 1967), *aff'd en banc sub nom,* Smuck v. Hobson, 408 F.2d 175 (D.C. Cir. 1969).
11. *Stewart v. Phillips,* Civil No. 70-1199-F (D. Mass., filed Sept. 14, 1970).

REFERENCES

American Psychological Association. Ethical standards of psychologists. *American Psychologist,* 1963, *18,* 56–60.

Becker, H. C. The nature of a profession. In N. B. Nelson (Ed.) *The sixty-first yearbook of the National Society for the Study of Education.* Chicago: NSSE, 1962.

Bersoff, D. N. Coercion and reciprocity in psychotherapy. In C. T. Fischer & S. Brodsky (Eds.), *The Prometheus principle: Informed participation by clients in human services.* New Brunswick: Transaction, in press.

Bersoff, D. N. The ethical practice of school psychology: A rebuttal and suggested model. *Professional Psychology,* 1973, *4,* 305–312.

Department of Health, Education, and Welfare. Privacy rights of parents and students. *Federal Register,* January 6, 1975, *40,* 1208–1216.

Erikson, K. T. A comment on disguised observation in sociology. *Social Problems,* 1967, *14,* 366–373.

Fischer, C. T. The testee as co-evaluator. *Journal of Counseling Psychology,* 1970, *17,* 70–76.

Fleming, J. G., & Maximov, B. The patient or his victim: The therapist's dilemma. *California Law Review,* 1974, *62,* 1025–1068.

Foster, H., & Freed, D. J. A bill of rights for children. *Family Law Quarterly,* 1972, *6,* 343–375.

Friedson, E. *The profession of medicine.* New York: Dodd, Mead, 1970.

Fox, R. *Experiment perilous.* Glencoe, Ill.: The Free Press, 1959.

Goldman, L. Psychological secrecy and openness in the public schools. *Professional Psychology,* 1972, *3,* 370–374.

Holt, J. *Escape from childhood.* New York: E. P. Dutton, 1974.

Katz, J. *Experimentation with human beings.* New York: Russell Sage Foundation, 1972.

Kleinfeld, A. Balance of power among infants, their parents, and the state (I, II, III). *Family Law Quarterly,* 1970, 1971, *4, 5,* 320–349, 410–443, 64–107.

McClelland, D. C. Testing for competence rather than for "intelligence." *American Psychologist,* 1973, *28,* 1–14.

McDermott, P. A. Law, liability, and the school psychologist: Systems of law, privileged communication, and access to records. *Journal of School Psychology,* 1972, *10,* 299–305.

Nettler, G. Test burning in Texas. *American Psychologist,* 1959, *14,* 682–683.

Note, Parental consent requirements and privacy rights of minors: The contraceptive controversy. *Harvard Law Review,* 1975, *88,* 1001–1020.

Note, Counseling the counselors: Legal implications of counseling minors without parental consent. *Maryland Law Review,* 1971, *31,* 332–354.

Recent Cases. Constitutional Law–right of privacy–personality test used by school to identify potential drug abusers without informed consent of parents violates student's and parents' right of privacy. *Vanderbilt Law Review,* 1974, *27,* 372–381.

Roston, R. A. Ethical uncertainties and "technical" validities. *Professional Psychology,* 1975, *6,* 50–54.

Ruebhausen, O. M., & Brim, O. G. Privacy and behavioral research. *Columbia Law Review,* 1965, *65,* 1184–1215.

Sheerer, C. W., & Roston, R. A. Some legal and psychological concerns about personality testing in the public schools. *Federal Bar Journal,* 1971, *30,* 111–118.

Simmons, S., Monahan, J., Whiteley, R., & Whiteley, J. California court ruling on dangerousness stirs controversy. *APA Monitor,* March, 1975, *6,* 12, 18.

Szasz, T. S., & Hollander, M. H. A contribution to the philosophy of medicine–The basic models of doctor-patient relationships. *Archives of Internal Medicine,* 1956, *97,* 585–592.

Trachtman, G. M. Pupils, parents, privacy, and the school psychologist. *American Psychologist,* 1972, *27,* 37–45.

Wald, P. Making sense out of the rights of youth. *Human Rights,* 1974, *4,* 13–29.

Ziskin, J. *Coping with psychiatric and psychological testimony.* Beverly Hills: Law and Psychology Press, 1975.

Donald N. Bersoff
Yale Law School
New Haven, Connecticut

Journal of School Psychology
1975. • Vol. 13, No. 4

LAW, PROFESSIONAL PRACTICE, AND UNIVERSITY PREPARATION: WHERE DO WE GO FROM HERE?

BARTELL W. CARDON

University of Pennsylvania

Summary: In this time of legal decisions which call much professional practice into question, it is well to ask ourselves questions as to why we are the object of court concern and how our preparation is related to our difficulties. It is suggested that current psychological practice is basically Aristotelian in nature and that our specialty suffers as a consequence. Several suggestions are presented for adjustments in university preparation. Intelligence testing and ability grouping are referred to throughout, for they have been primary targets of the courts. Examples pertaining to personality and other often measured psychological variables could have as appropriately been offered.

There is something very distinctive about our specialty which separates it from all other branches of psychology and psychiatry—school psychology has elected to work within schools and within educational objectives. Ours is the task of applying theories, notions, strategies, and tools of psychology to education so that children and youth will be schooled to their best advantage.

To identify with education presents its own risks for, today as never before, the schools are experiencing severe attack from all sides—students, parents, educators, and self proclaimed "experts." It is in no way surprising that school psychology finds itself increasingly stage center, in full view of those who see folly, injustice, and misguided goals and procedures in contemporary education.

Although there is considerable discomfort in being a target of criticism and at times of outright hostility, there is little gain in putting one's head in the sand hoping that the spotlight of attention will swing elsewhere. Felt pain is much like a flashing yellow light, to be responded to by slowing and looking both ways to determine if it is advantageous to proceed. Such is our condition now as an unholy(?) cacaphony of dissonent voices is reaching and swaying the courts.

A question warrants repeated asking in the face of legal decisions which influence our professional practices. It is this: "What are the courts saying to us as we sell our wares in the schools?" Removing all the legal trappings, it would appear that there are three serious challenges being put before us. A review of legal interpretations which interface with psychological services within education results in the obvious conclusion that both our psychometric approach to referral concerns and our assessment based recommendations are being called into question. Less apparent, but much more important ultimately, is the challenge to our philosophical-theoretical assumptions.

PHILOSOPHICAL ORIENTATION

In his classic 1931 article, "The Conflict Between Aristotelian Galilean Modes of Thought in Contemporary Psychology," Kurt Lewin attempted to make war with philosophical currents within psychology which were fundamentally Aristotelian in nature. Judging from present practices, it would appear that his "cry in the wilderness" has not been responded to (if even heard) in any significant way by the majority of psychologists working within the educational enterprise.

To present an extended comparison between Aristotelian and other modes of thinking is a temptation which must be put aside in the interest of brevity. A few general comments will, of necessity, suffice.

Aristotelian thought has several cardinal characteristics. First, classification is permitted, if not insisted upon. Second, membership within any given abstract class is considered to define the "essence" or "tendency" (sum of characteristics shared or essential nature) of the individual members, as reflected in lawful and predictable behavior. Third, classification usually results in opposites, abstract classes which are *valuative* in nature.

When a child is referred to the psychologist because of academic difficulty, the ensuing steps are often somewhat as follows: (1) administer a WISC-R or Binet (among others), (2) determine an intellectual level (IQ), then (3) recommend placement in a class for educable mentally retarded children. Compare this process with the aforementioned characteristics of Aristotelian thought.

The psychologist applies an instrument for the purpose of classifying (the assumption that classification is appropriate and "good" underrides this act), derives an IQ (which must denote "essence" or "tendency" for it facilitates the next step), recommends separation of this "class" of child from the other class (i.e., acts as if children are either retarded or not retarded).

Kuriloff (Note 1) has portrayed this process in poignant fashion by conceptualizing the school psychologist as an active employee of a large Sunkist packing plant. "Psychometric criteria correspond to the various sized holes in the conveyor belt. Children, like fruit, pass along the belt until they drop through the appropriately sized holes (IQ levels) and thence to chutes which in turn terminate in boxes (curricula) variously labelled, for example: U. S. Grade Triple A, college bound; U. S. Grade A Small, business track; or U. S. Grade B Damaged, educably retarded—for clinical use only (the latter children, like bruised and damaged fruit, are only suitable for canning)" (p.5).

The ubiquitous valuative (good vs. bad) characteristic of Aristotelian classification is clearly seen today in our attitudes and "remedial" responses to children who are "retardates," "underachievers," and "perceptually impaired," as opposed to those who are found to be "normal," "achievers," and "perceptually intact," as examples.

This extremely brief presentation of Aristotelian thought and of the behavior and assumptions of school psychologists is admittedly simplistic. But, the point to be made is that "the concepts of [school] psychology, at least in certain decisive respects, are thoroughly Aristotelian in their actual content, even though in many respects their form of presentation has been somewhat 'civilized,' so to speak" (Lewin, 1930, p.151).

A close look at court rulings which impinge upon school psychology unmasks a fascinating philosophical confrontation. In effect, the courts are mandating an educational system or process which must be, by definition, hostile climate for Aristotelian psychologists.

PSYCHOLOGICAL INSTRUMENTATION

It would be expected that our philosophical stance is reflected in our tools, both in terms of what variables are being measured by the instruments we are prone to employ and the forms and characteristics of the data emanating from their use. This is clearly so when considering measures of intelligence, a major target of the courts. Much has been written for and against intelligence testing, and to add more would belabor the controversy. However, several points are particularly germane to our interplay with the courts.

There are three courses of action which can be taken educationally on the basis of intellectual assessment: (1) do nothing; (2) adjust the educational strategies and materials to which the child is exposed; and/or (3) place the child in a special setting. In reality, the second process is seldom if ever undertaken. This is largely due to the nature of the intelligence measures used.

Group instruments normally provide (at best) three IQ's—a verbal IQ, a performance IQ, and a combined or general IQ. A basic problem of such indicators is that although they provide a numerical statement regarding where a child stands intellectually in relation to his or her peers, they do not offer information as to specific strengths or weaknesses. These tests are not intended to provide remedial information. Their primary purpose is that of screening out (categorizing) children who can be expected to experience difficulty in the academic setting.

It is precisely the absence of diagnostic value found in such tests that led to the development of instruments (such as the WISC-R) which generate multiple scores. Unfortunately, these multiple scores have not supplied educators with much diagnostic or remedial advantage. As was true of the more global indices, the subscale scores reflect relative standings of the child to his or her immediate peers (assuming that local norms are used, which almost never happens), but do not provide information regarding learning-instructional strengths or weaknesses. Without such information, remediation is not a natural extension of these subscale data. Consequently, it must be assumed that the instruments are, in the final analysis, "predictive devices and nothing more" (Reger, 1966).

The courts have recognized that the tests are predictive, but they have not been overly sympathetic with the assumption that they *have to be* predictive. The schools are being told to compensate for that which results in certain groups (Blacks, Chicanos, etc.) being overrepresented among children considered as likely to not fare well within regular education. We, the psychologists, are being told (although not so directly) to readdress our psychometric attention to variables of more direct educational relevance than "intelligence." At an even more subtle level, we are being asked to reconsider our views of "essence" or "tendency."

PSYCHOLOGICAL RECOMMENDATIONS

Just as our tools would be expected to reflect our philosophical assumptions, so our recommendations could be anticipated to be an extension of our tools. Although psychology can demonstrate most convincingly that intelligence test data are often highly predictive of future academic success, there are at least two serious difficulties which seem to be down played when a decision is made to place a referred child or youth in a class for the mentally retarded.

First, the predictability of a test can be conceptualized as an "all-things-being-equal" state. That is to say, predictability exists as long as contaminating intervention is not present. We know this and make our recommendations with the anticipation that special placement will "overturn" the expected. But what is often overlooked is that the predictability of intelligence test data endorses neither the notion of classification nor the educational practice of ability grouping.

Second, psychologists have long known that predictability (in the statistical sense) is a *group* phenomenon. For any given member of a group, however, the question of predictability is not the same as it is for the group of which (s)he is part. Whereas there will be significantly more "hits" than "misses" when making academic prediction (on the basis of IQ's) about a group of children, the psychologist will be either right or wrong (in the relative rather than absolute sense) when dealing with a single child.

Just why these two issues have become millstones about our necks is explained in the assumptions we make. Although the fact that intelligence and achievement are correlated does not lead intrinsically to classification schemes or to the practice of ability grouping, we *assume* that it does. Our penchant for categorizing people and things shows through. Although the placing of a child in special education represents either a "hit" or a "miss," we *assume* all "hits," which may explain, at least in part, why it was the courts which have pushed us into the "re-eval" business. Our tendency to ascribe commonality to members of a class is apparent, or so it would appear.

What, then, can be said of these placement recommendations wherein children and youth are grouped by intellectual levels? In 1968, 50 studies considered to be the best available were reviewed by the National Educational Association. Table 1 presents the conclusions of the review (as reported by Jencks, 1972).

Table 1
Number* of Studies Showing Various Effects of Ability Grouping upon Achievement

Ability Level of Students	Favorable Effects	Mixed Effects	Unfavorable or Insignificant Effects
Talented	18	11	17
Average	11	12	10
Slow	12	10	17

*The total will exceed 50, the number of studies examined, as some studies evaluated more than one ability level.

It is immediately apparent that an important generalization can be drawn on the basis of these data, a generalization which is supported by other more recent reviews of the ability grouping literature (e.g., Findley & Bryan, 1971, we cannot predict the outcomes of ability grouping to any significant degree. The single safest statement which can be made is that ability grouping appears to be more unfavorable or nonsignificant in its influence upon slow students than is true for average and talented students.

IQs when used as current status indicators for placement purposes have not provided education with predictable outcomes. Despite years of experience with special education and other forms of ability grouping, we find ourselves, for one reason or another, unable to say with any assurance that children are advantaged as a result of these educational groupings. Clearly, the courts are emphasizing the disadvantages of classification by intellectual status.

WHERE DO WE GO FROM HERE?

There is an everflowing stream of articles in our journals decrying the unhappy conditions of school psychological services. Papers with similar themes are annually presented at national, regional, and local conventions. The articles and papers bear a common thread, the vast majority come from university affiliated psychologists. It is an interesting paradox, if one accepts the proposition that university preparation makes a difference, that the professional practice of school psychology should be criticized by the very individuals who bring the practitioners into being. (It needs to be quickly noted that to say that the preponderance of criticism comes from university affiliated psychologists it *not* to suggest that most university psychologists are involved in such criticism.)

Perhaps it is the universities which must accept much of the responsibility for the difficulties currently being experienced by the practitioners. It is very possible that preparation programs are educating school psychologists in ways which insure that directly and indirectly they must ultimately find themselves targets of the courts.

Based upon the assumption that the professional practice of school psychology is a reflection of academic preparation, and that a major responsibility of the academic school psychologist is to provide theoretical-practical leadership for the specialty, focus will be upon what universities might consider as alternatives or enhancements to current programming.

Philosophical Re-orientation. There is a curious and troublesome relationship between many school psychologists and their work. Although Kuriloff's Sunkist packing plant analogy to our interaction with children and youth is patently offensive to us, for we generally disassociate ourselves from such blatant pigeonholing, the fact remains that it is an all too accurate reflection of what is happening in the schools and of that with which the courts are now taking exception. The offense of the analogy is not in being unjustly accused of something we do not do, but in having to face either the unhappy outcomes of thinking and acting in Aristotelian ways or the *disparity* between what we do and what we believe, or think we believe, we should be doing.

Although school psychologists face many obstacles in their work, the position taken here is that the single most impactful hindrance, the one which if overcome would smooth out many, if not most, of the wrinkles in the fabric of our interaction with public education and the courts, is directly related to our philosophical preparation, or lack of it.

It is a rare training program which provides the fledgling school psychologist with even the most superficial exposure to the philosoph*ies* of science (psychology) and education. Even more uncommon is the formal attempt to assist the budding psychologist in building a philosophical orientation which is in harmony with his or her basic and deep seated personal, religious and social beliefs. It is this combined program weakness which may ultimately be found to be having stiltifying impact upon our specialty, for a professional psychologist whose beliefs and practice are in disharmony, or are unrelated, is much like an individual attempting to drive a Cadillac using pancake syrup as fuel.

The universities could do much to improve the philosophical preparation of psychologists who must face the realities of the educational enterprise. Recommended is a three pronged approach which represents an integration of philosophical content across all coursework and experiences.

Basic philosophy. Although one can sympathize with the pressures put upon school psychology educators to get the most done in the usually short time available, one must question the ultimate value of placing program emphasis upon skills (e.g., psychometrics, behavior modification, etc.) at the expense of penetrating exposure to philosophy and theory. To function competently in the field, psychologists must not only possess an understanding of varying views of the world and its dynamics but must also be assisted to know that *each* professional tool—be it theory, classification and diagnostic instrumentation, or any given remediational strategy—is ladened with philosophical implications and assumptions, and that the psychological and educational outcomes of using any particular tool are, consequently, predictable.

Philosophical consistency. It is not enough, however, to send students through a course or two emphasizing philosophy. Programs should strive to insure philosophical consistency *within* the individual. Because students come to any given program within varying belief and assumption systems, it may be more important to strive for individual rather than program integrity. Just how this is accomplished, whether through coursework, seminars, or individual effort, is not as important as that students be formally introduced to the need of bringing personal belief systems and professional ethical and philosophical-theoretical systems into harmony, and that structures exist to facilitate such an endeavor.

Justification. Students would be greatly advantaged if training programs were to institute "justification" procedures wherein they, the students, would be routinely expected to justify in terms of philosophy, theory, objectives, and the like, each phase of school related psychological service. This would create habits of professional service based upon the premise that similarities across problem situations do not necessarily justify uniform or standard psychological response. It would also assist the school psychologist to guard against the use of tools and strategies not harmonious with his or her philosophical base. Such philosophical questioning would greatly increase the likelihood that we will more skillfully "look before we leap."

Psycho-Educational Instrumentation. We are increasingly finding ourselves in what appear to be "no win," double bind situations. Take, for instance, the clash of the state mandated classification role of the school psychologist with court decisions which seem to be in contradiction. We are damned if we classify and damned if we don't, at least that's the way it appears to many of us.

When the courts rule against grouping by IQ, they do so because they desire that children and youth be educationally advantaged and consider such grouping procedures to be detrimental. When the state departments of education mandate in favor of grouping by IQ, they do so becuase they desire that children and youth be educationally advantaged and consider such grouping procedures to be beneficial. How is it that antithetical educational procedures (ability grouping vs. nonability grouping) are being supported by institutions (schools and courts) which have the same basic objectives (safeguarding children)?

The answer, or at least one answer, may be that the schools and the courts are working under differing assumptions. Schools, administratively at least, seek to find commonality in students to permit grouping for educational purposes. "Essence" or "tendency" is emphasized; individual differences are minimized. The courts, on the other hand, find in favor of those who wish that individual uniqueness be stressed and against systems which emphasize grouping along "essence" or "tendency" dimensions.

Now as long as classification is a point of confrontation between schools and courts, the school psychologist will continue to be positioned in the crossfire of differing modes of conceptualizing what is educationally best for children. *One* alternative is to reconceptualize the notion of classification in such a way that it is neither necessary to classify nor to not classify children and youth in order to assist them educationally.

An example of this would be to stress the process through which students must pass in the school with diminished regard to the "essence" or "tendency" of groups. To do this would require instrumentation, among other things, which focuses more upon status within the process than upon personal characteristics such as general intelligence.

The courts have ruled that ability grouping is inherently prejudicial in that it results in de facto segregation due to the over-representation of minority children and youth in classes for the retarded. Mainstreaming (which will soon present us with difficulties which will make our current plight appear as minor) appears to be the courts' solution. Yet one gains the very strong impression when studying the complaints of opponents to special education that their real concern is not that of education attempting to provide assistance to children and youth with special needs via special educational techniques (including grouping), but that children are being grouped along *non*-educational variables (e.g., intelligence) which have powerful social meaning. Members of minority groups readily admit to academic difficulties, but not to intellectual inferiority. In spite of protestations to the contrary by psychologists, intelligence is generally considered to be an integral and unvariable part of the individual rather than a changeable reflection of an interaction of nature and nurture. It should not be in any way unexpected that minorities, and the courts as a consequence, are upset that notions and measures of intelligence are part of education.

Herein is the beauty of academically based criterion referenced assessment and diagnostic measurement. Students are viewed, or the potential for such viewing is greater, in terms of achievement centered variables (what they can do, what they know) rather than in terms of non-educational variables (what they are). Criterion referenced measures have many advantages over norm referenced instruments in that the latter encourage the users to fall into Aristotelian assumption and strategy traps. The use of criterion referenced assessment techniques, and of some of the better diagnostic instruments, does not require classification into groups as a remediational strategy, nor does it preclude such procedures. When using these instruments, the issue of grouping ceases to be central for the psychologist. Even more important, the controversial focus upon intelligence could be put aside.

It can be argued rather forcefully that merely changing instruments is not going to lead to changes in consequence. This is correct. If a psychologist wishes to impose Aristotelian assumptions upon his or her work, then there is little reason to expect much difference in outcomes. That is not the point. Rather, what is being suggested is that if a psychologist desires to function in a *non*-Aristotelian manner, then s(he) will be considerably disadvantaged by using instrumentation which is blantantly Aristotelian in design and intent.

Here again the universities may play a very significant role in assisting the school psychologist. A close look at most training programs uncovers a rather common "core" program in assessment: a course in measurement (usually statistical in content), a course in individual mental measurement (with heavy commitment to the WISC-R, WPPSI, Binet), a course in personality assessment (focusing upon the TAT, CAT, Rorschach, sentence completion, Bender), and a survey course (possibly) of other instruments. Increasingly, there is added to the above some coursework in "learning disabilities." Surprisingly few programs expect more than symbolic diagnostic and remediation expertise in basic academic areas such as reading, mathematics, and the like.

The heavy emphasis is upon individual assessment of variables such as intelligence, personality, and "minimal cerebral dysfunction" employing instruments which are designed to classify either directly via statistical norming or more indirectly through underriding theoretical constructs such as neurosis, mental retardation, and so forth.

In the eyes of a non-Aristotelian psychologist, then, it would appear as if school psychologists receive significant exposure to relatively useless instruments (in terms of educational outcomes) and rather superficial contact with those which might better serve the needs of students and educators. What may be needed is more opportunity for students to be exposed to alternative assessment notions, notions not tied to group tendency, for instance.

Psychological-Educational Foundations. At our best, we are knowledgeable and contributing resource specialists to educators. We apply sound psychological insights and tools appropriately within the schools. We recommend educational alternatives designed to enhance a student's position within the educational process.

Unfortunately, we are not always at our best, for the educational outcomes of some of our major undertakings (e.g., ability grouping) have proven an embarrassment to us as the current gatekeepers of special education. Our emphasis upon intelligence testing and special placements has distracted us from countless alternative possibilities.

Some critics suspect that we continue as we do, not so much because we believe in what we are doing as because to behave differently would force us into a position even more uncomfortable than the one now experienced. That position if one of having to propose strategies and offer recommendations which are by their very nature educationally based. It is further suggested that most school psychologists are not well grounded in either psychological or educational theory and practice to the point of permitting easy transition.

Even were we well prepared as psychologists, we would experience considerable difficulty without deep foundations in education. Many of us might be surprised to find that a major wellspring from which we might draw sound psychologically based recommendations is educational theory and practice.

Are the universities providing adequate exposure to education both as a profession and as a process (or processes)? Do we enter the field with an understanding of educational systems sufficient to permit us to introduce needed change? Do we have the necessary expertise to propose alternative methods of educational groupings which do not suffer the limitations of ability grouping? Are we introduced to the vast wealth of educational know-how which has accumulated over decades, if not centuries? Probably not, and herein is an area of preparation which merits serious attention on the part of educators of school psychologists.

CONCLUSIONS

Some will say that what we now are doing in the schools is not of our choosing or under our control, that we aren't in a position to dictate what shall be measured or for what reasons. The retort to such a claim is simple: if we are mandated to use the instruments (and assumptions) which *we* introduced into the educational world in years past, then there is little reason to suspect that we cannot be mandated to use other instruments (and assumptions) which we now wish to have introduced.

The heart of the problem we face is not whether we can introduce alternative forms of psychological services (leading to alternative forms of educational opportunities for students), for there is ample evidence that we can. The basic issue is: are we being provided a comfortable philosophical-theoretical base (including tools and strategies) for alternative service?

REFERENCE NOTE

1. Kuriloff, P. *The Impact of Aristotelian Thinking: A Call for Change in the Way School Psychologists Conceptualize Educational Problems* (Unpublished manuscript, 1973).

REFERENCES

Findley, W. G. & Bryan, M. M. *Ability Grouping: 1970.* Athens, Ga.: Center for Educational Improvement, University of Georgia, 1971.

Jencks, C. *Inequality: A Reassessment of the Effects of Family and Schooling in America.* New York: Basic Books, 1972.

Lewin, K. The Conflict Between Aristotelian and Galilean Modes of Thought in Contemporary Psychology. *Journal of General Psychology,* 1931, *5,* 141–177.

Reger, R. Myths About Intelligence. *Journal of School Psychology,* 1966, 3, 39–44.

Bartell W. Cardon
Associate Professor of Education
Graduate School of Education
University of Pennsylvania
Philadelphia, Pennsylvania 19174

U. S. POSTAL SERVICE
STATEMENT OF OWNERSHIP, MANAGEMENT AND CIRCULATION
(Act of August 12, 1970: Section 3685. Title 39. United States Code)

1. TITLE OF PUBLICATION: JOURNAL OF SCHOOL PSYCHOLOGY
2. DATE OF FILING: Sept. 19, 1975
3. FREQUENCY OF ISSUE: QUATERLY
3A. ANNUAL SUBSCRIPTION PRICE: $12 Indiv/$35 Inst
4. LOCATION OF KNOWN OFFICE OF PUBLICATION *(Street, city, county, state and ZIP code) (Not printers)*: 72 Fifth Ave. NY.,N.Y. 10011
5. LOCATION OF THE HEADQUARTERS OR GENERAL BUSINESS OFFICES OF THE PUBLISHERS *(Not printers)*: 72 Fifth Ave. NY.,N.Y. 10011
6. NAMES AND ADDRESSES OF PUBLISHER, EDITOR, AND MANAGING EDITOR

PUBLISHER *(Name and address)*: Behavioral Publications, Inc., 72 Fifth Ave. N.Y.,N.Y. 10011
EDITOR *(Name and address)*: Beeman N. Phillips, The University of Texas, College of Education, Dept of Educational Psy. Austin ,Texas 78712
MANAGING EDITOR *(Name and address)*: Judith Ornstein, Behavioral Publications, Inc.,72 Fifth Ave, NY.,N.Y.,

7. OWNER *(If owned by a corporation, its name and address must be stated and also immediately thereunder the names and addresses of stockholders owning or holding 1 percent or more of total amount of stock. If not owned by a corporation, the names and addresses of the individual owners must be given. If owned by a partnership or other unincorporated firm, its name and address, as well as that of each individual must be given.)*

NAME	ADDRESS
Journal of School Psychology, Inc.	The University of Akron Akron, Ohio 44325

8. KNOWN BONDHOLDERS, MORTGAGEES, AND OTHER SECURITY HOLDERS OWNING OR HOLDING 1 PERCENT OR MORE OF TOTAL AMOUNT OF BONDS, MORTGAGES OR OTHER SECURITIES *(If there are none, so state)*

NAME	ADDRESS
none	

9. FOR OPTIONAL COMPLETION BY PUBLISHERS MAILING AT THE REGULAR RATES *(Section 132.121, Postal Service Manual)*

39 U. S. C. 3626 provides in pertinent part: "No person who would have been entitled to mail matter under former section 4359 of this title shall mail such matter at the rates provided under this subsection unless he files annually with the Postal Service a written request for permission to mail matter at such rates."

In accordance with the provisions of this statute, I hereby request permission to mail the publication named in Item 1 at the reduced postage rates presently authorized by 39 U. S. C. 3626.

(Signature and title of editor, publisher, business manager, or owner) Judith A. Ornstein

10. FOR COMPLETION BY NONPROFIT ORGANIZATIONS AUTHORIZED TO MAIL AT SPECIAL RATES *(Section 132.122 Postal Service Manual) (Check one)*

The purpose, function, and nonprofit status of this organization and the exempt status for Federal income tax purposes ☐ Have not changed during preceding 12 months ☐ Have changed during preceding 12 months *(If changed, publisher must submit explanation of change with this statement.)*

11. EXTENT AND NATURE OF CIRCULATION	AVERAGE NO. COPIES EACH ISSUE DURING PRECEDING 12 MONTHS	ACTUAL NUMBER OF COPIES OF SINGLE ISSUE PUBLISHED NEAREST TO FILING DATE
A. TOTAL NO. COPIES PRINTED *(Net Press Run)*	3050	3,100
B. PAID CIRCULATION 1. SALES THROUGH DEALERS AND CARRIERS, STREET VENDORS AND COUNTER SALES	none	none
2. MAIL SUBSCRIPTIONS	2,733	2,525
C. TOTAL PAID CIRCULATION	2,733	2,525
D. FREE DISTRIBUTION BY MAIL, CARRIER OR OTHER MEANS SAMPLES, COMPLIMENTARY, AND OTHER FREE COPIES	65	65
E. TOTAL DISTRIBUTION *(Sum of C and D)*	2,798	2,590
F. COPIES NOT DISTRIBUTED 1. OFFICE USE, LEFT-OVER, UNACCOUNTED, SPOILED AFTER PRINTING	252	510
2. RETURNS FROM NEWS AGENTS	none	none
G. TOTAL *(Sum of E & F—should equal net press run shown in A)*	3,050	3,100

I certify that the statements made by me above are correct and complete. SIGNATURE OF EDITOR, PUBLISHER, BUSINESS MANAGER, OR OWNER: Judith A. Ornstein

PS Form Jan 1975 3526 (Page 1) *(See instructions on reverse)*